LINDA EVANS

Also by Michael Freedland

Peter O'Toole
The Warner Brothers
Jack Lemmon
The Secret Life of Danny Kaye

MICHAEL FREEDLAND

LINDA EVANS

St. Martin's Press
New York

Illustration Acknowledgments

The photographs in this book are reproduced by kind permission of the following:

The Kobal Collection 2, 11, 16; *Napthine-Walsh Collections* 3, 4, 5 above; *Rex Features* 9, 10, 17 below, 18, 19, 23; *Scope Features* 1 above, 6, 7, 12, 13, 20 below, 21, 24; *Frank Spooner–Gamma* 14, 15, 22; *Syndication International* 1 below, 5 below, 8, 17 above, 20 above.

LINDA EVANS. Copyright © 1986 by Michael Freedland. All rights reserved. Printed in the United States of America. No part of this book may be used or reproduced in any manner whatsoever without written permission except in the case of brief quotations embodied in critical articles or reviews. For information, address St. Martin's Press, 175 Fifth Avenue, New York, N.Y. 10010.

Library of Congress Cataloging in Publication Data

Freedman, Michael, 1934–
  Linda Evans.

  I. Evans, Linda, 1942–   . 2. Actors—
United States—Biography. I. Title.
PN2287.E78F7   1987   791.45′028′0924   [B]   86-24836
ISBN 0-312-00151-7

First published in Great Britain by George Weidenfeld & Nicolson Limited.

First U.S. Edition

10 9 8 7 6 5 4 3 2 1

LINDA EVANS

Introduction

This is the story of a little girl who dreamed of being a princess but who ended up with a Dynasty; of a woman who didn't pretend to be young but who stood up to be counted when the call came for all forty-year-olds to identify themselves.

Sophie Tucker could never have imagined just how much life began at forty. Linda Evans was born into a generation when the great stars were the Cary Grants and the Lana Turners. Garbo had already made her last film, *Two-Faced Woman*, the year before and Fred Astaire had all but ended his partnership with Ginger Rogers (and was busy trying out a new one with an actress called Rita Hayworth).

Now a lot of what those names represented has been reincarnated in this television heiress.

She has never pretended to be a great actress, yet together with her close colleague - and senior by about ten years – Joan Collins, she is the nearest thing to a star of the old school thrown up by the television generation of the 1980s.

Linda wears dresses with huge shoulders and so dresses with huge shoulders become fashionable. Her necklines plunge and so do the sales of clothes with high necks. Her hair is silvery blonde shaped into a square bob, and any day in any suburban shopping centre in any one of a hundred Western countries, you'll see women who don't pretend to be less than forty with hair as close to her style as their neighbourhood hairdressers can make it.

That's stardom. That's style. It may be a contrived kind of

5

stardom, a man-made style, a hyped operation of the kind used to sell perfume – she's done that, too, in her time – but it had been known to work before and in the extraordinary shape of Miss Linda Evans it is working again.

Linda Evans has become a queen of that brand of television which is unfortunately called 'soap'. Not a new term, for when Linda was born there were 'soap operas' on the radio. But the bubbles her soap has created have long left the world of TV behind.

That in itself is an achievement. But what else has she achieved? Probably most of all to be the kind of woman other women want to be. And that isn't just because of the clothes she wears – never as outlandish or extreme as those adopted by Miss Collins. Nor even because of the make-up she applies – she has frequently been seen with apparently none at all on her face. And certainly it is not because of the money and the home that it bought – most women who eye Linda Evans enviously see the mansion in Denver, Colorado, as little more than a museum.

But to have that apparent self assurance; to be loved by a fabulously successful man with a blue rinse; to look so feminine, yet so forty-plus, has to be something to envy and admire.

Ask Linda herself about her achievements and her success and she'll play coy – at the same time giving the impression that she can smooth over any difficulties that might occasionally arise in her life as effectively as she tells her cook how many she expects for dinner at the mansion.

Try to seek explanations from her and she'll tell you that she is still too young to do anything of the kind. Life does really, in her case, begin at forty.

To her she's in the midst of childhood. Second childhood perhaps, but without pretending to be anyone's doll. She shows you can be mature, have a late baby (on screen) and still have that magic insouciance men find so attractive.

Her millions – and that is no exaggeration – of fans see a woman with many loves – many lives, some may think – who, though, has had her share of regrets, of disappointments, of traumas.

But the gaps in her life are not the ones that people think about. They are not of the stuff that hinders a career which became outstanding, if only because it blossomed so late.

One doesn't have to be a fan of soap operas to realise this. One doesn't even have to enjoy *Dynasty* to appreciate that Linda Evans has taken off quite as much as the oil that ostensibly fueled her and her TV husband's wealth.

Miss Evans, on the other hand, has burst forth with all the energy that the oil is expected to generate. In fact, the story itself long ago became a mere adjunct to the characters. Women like Linda fulfil much the same sort of role as the songs in the old Hollywood musicals – the real reason for having the shows. The story line is made to fit around that bobbed hair and those padded shoulders.

Linda Evans is indeed a big, big star.

If only her parents could have imagined when she was born what would happen....

1

She was a Hollywood child. In a way, more of a Hollywood child than those juvenile products of the film factory star system, Shirley Temple, Judy Garland or Elizabeth Taylor. Linda Evanstad wasn't actually born in Hollywood, she was taken there by her parents when she was six months old – which is pretty well as close to being born there as most other stars could possibly claim.

Certainly, it was a more attractive place to have in her biography than Hartford, Connecticut, where she *was* born on 18 November 1942. (Psychologists might point to a slight coincidence there, certainly one that might register more effectively in a Trivial Pursuit game – Hartford was the home of that Life Begins At Forty star, Sophie Tucker.)

Changing the name to Evans would come later. Evanstad has the sound of Scandinavia about it – which doubtless explains that cool, blonde look which pierces its way out of the television screens. In fact, her father, Alba Evanstad, was of Norwegian descent.

Alba, if one was to believe the press releases, was a professional dancer – which only goes to prove that the old Hollywood philosophy of never telling the truth when a downright lie is more attractive has been a long time a-dying. She herself probably never knew about it – actors and actresses themselves are rarely consulted when mere details like supplying career material are being handled – but the studio handouts made it seem like she had show biz in the blood.

That is only true if the zeal with which he plastered wallpaper could be regarded as showmanship. Mr Evanstad was a painter and decorator, who took his family, his wife, their daughters Carol, Kathy and baby Linda to Hollywood in the hope that he would find more work. He reckoned no doubt that people in the movie business could afford to have their homes decorated more often than those in Hartford.

He had originally called himself an interior decorator, but before long he was throwing off all pretensions and admitting he was just a house painter – a house painter who didn't get much work.

He found it very difficult to make ends meet. But he gave the kids what he could and it was enough for Linda to admit to herself that she had a crush on him. As she said, 'I knew that I was competing with my mother for his attention. My father was quite a bit older than my mother.' Reflecting on what would happen to her a generation later, she said: 'It seems to be a pattern.'

The lack of money didn't have much effect on Linda. 'It never seemed to matter to me,' she said. But she didn't know the agony that doing without caused her parents. Of Alba, she said, 'It grieved him that he could never give his children the things other fathers gave theirs. But he gave himself to my sisters and me and that was the most important gift of all.' The Evanstads sent their daughters to Hollywood High School – the Alma Mater of a star of an earlier era, Lana Turner. Among those at the school at the same time were two other girls who achieved a measure of stardom themselves, Stefanie Powers and Tuesday Weld.

Linda became a member of the Beta Psi Delta sorority – the one which was traditionally reserved for the 'good girls'. She said that the indignity of that stayed with her for too long.

She confesses to this day that she was a pitifully shy girl – so shy that she was frightened to participate in any school activities. 'I was too shy even to read a book report in class at school,' she once recalled.

Linda was to say: 'My main purpose was to be loved. I was

frightened of rejection. I resigned myself to being passive and submissive at any cost.' It was a resignation which before long would get her seriously into trouble.

She was so shy that the impact she made on her fellow students was considerably less than that which she would later present to the fans of a certain TV show. 'I was here when Linda was a student,' one of the staff members there told me. 'But I have to be honest. I just don't remember her. She must have been very nice because the bad ones we always remember.'

But how nice? 'Oh Linda was fun,' said a Hollywood matron who shared packed lunches with her. 'But there isn't a lot to say about her. She was like a lot of the other kids. Very quiet. There was nothing about her that stands out in my memory.'

In fact, the principal of the school seems to have accepted that about her and been sufficiently worried about it to suggest that perhaps she ought to take up dramatics. She enrolled in the first drama class, and gradually built her way up to higher courses.

It wasn't a brilliant episode in Linda's career. In fact, she was so shy that the toughest thing for her to do was simply to walk from the wings on to the main stage. Her mother realised that – and also noticed the way she walked.

Mrs Evanstad suggested that Linda might like to consider modelling. She realised that a tall girl like her might not only find some self assurance by learning how to be a model but might also make a fairly good living. It was good advice and enrolling at the Flair Modelling School in Hollywood must go down as one of the soundest decisions made on Linda's behalf in those early formative years.

The enterprise appeared to have worked. Suddenly the shy young thing was of necessity having to operate in a world where there were real people, who wouldn't always be saying the nice, reassuring things that were said to her at home.

'I discovered I could handle myself in public,' she was to say years later. 'They taught me how to enter a room without feeling awkward or afraid.' It was self confidence she was after and now she was slowly discovering it was quite attainable for her.

She was a happy enough child. Everything at home seemed simple and pleasant. Her parents told her to be good, so good she became. 'Do what people say and they will love you,' her mother told her. So that became the rule by which she was to be guided.

They gathered around the piano each night, mother, father, three daughters, and sang the songs of the time. Linda, however, seems to have had more pleasure from singing than the rest of the family did from hearing her.

'Who's off-key?' one of the girls said to her one evening and Linda was so upset by that event that she vowed there and then that no one would ever hear her singing a song again. If she did sing, it would be to herself, in the confines of a bathroom perhaps. And it was a vow she kept until she was much, much older.

But it upset her. She loved to sing. Not being able to do so seemed to the young child Linda to be an immense deprivation. And she never forgot it.

What she never felt deprived of was the love and care of her parents. Her father didn't even give her a time to be home at night. As she was to say: 'I must have been the oldest virgin in Hollywood.' She said that when she was forty-two and starring in *Dynasty* – and was referring to the time when she was fifteen, which either means there was a great deal of poetic licence in the story she was telling or else the permissive age really had struck Hollywood a lot earlier than even the historians have recorded. However, it was fairly clear what she meant. 'When I was a teenager, all my girl friends had a curfew. My Dad just said, "You'll know when to come home".'

Her parents were strict Roman Catholics and that was how they brought up their daughter. She went to Mass, took Holy Communion. But the indoctrination of the Church didn't last. It was not that she was no longer a believer in God, but the style of Catholicism lost its appeal. To some who go on to make their careers in show business, the very theatricality of the

Church has a tremendous appeal. It didn't have that effect on Linda.

Indeed, as she burst into a beautiful puberty, with high firm breasts, pleasantly rounded hips and the kind of legs the principal of the modelling school secretly boasted of to visitors, religion no longer had any drawing power.

The events leading up to her fifteenth birthday could have had something to do with it. Her father became ill. Before long, Mrs Evanstad confided to her daughters that Alba had cancer. He was going to die.

It was one of the most traumatic times of her life and one she will never forget – although for as much as twenty years that was precisely what she tried to do.

And that attitude started while he was still lying in bed.

'I was unable to cope with this,' she was to say. 'So I blocked it out. I pretended that my father had to stay in bed for a while, but that eventually he'd be fine.'

It was the kind of reaction many another child – and not a few fully-grown adults – will easily recognise. Coping with the certainty of death is the hardest part of life.

It also released a factor in Linda's own existence which had long haunted her – her sense of impatience. Being patient had never been a Linda Evans quality. Now, though, it was manifesting itself in a strange way. She suddenly became impatient for him to die. That wasn't as callous an emotion as may immediately strike the eye. She was impatient with his suffering and wanted it to be over. 'It was very difficult for me to watch him. I wanted him to die so he wouldn't suffer any more.'

It is something that has lingered. As she says: 'I'm still impatient with suffering and illness. I want to fix it so everybody will get well right away.'

When her father did actually die, she decided that the best thing was to try to ignore it. Not to pretend that he was still there, lying in bed at home, but that the whole episode hadn't occurred at all. It was easier than being brave and coping with an unpalatable event in life.

Not trying to cope is nature's own anaesthetic. For Linda, the traumatisation and the numbness lasted long after the effects of that anaesthetic were expected to wear off.

She summed it up very neatly for herself. 'My innermost feelings started attacking me. Had I been there for him? Did he know how much I loved him? What should I have said to him that I couldn't say now.'

They might have been the feelings others share, but that fact did not reduce the horror of having to face them. As she said, 'A part of me felt that I had abandoned my father. Whatever lessons I should have learned from his death were ignored because the pain and the guilt were too much for me to bear. I immediately buried the entire experience.'

The experience stayed buried with her father's body. The feelings she suffered were not to be exhumed until she was thirty years old and suddenly felt able to cope with them.

But it was probably because she had, in fact, buried those feelings that she was able to cope with life as it was. The anaesthetic kept one corner of her emotions sufficiently numb for her to enjoy talking to her classmates, discovering something of the opposite sex – she liked them as much as they evidently liked her – and of the kind of world which existed outside the confines of her home or schools.

It was Carole Wells, a friend of hers who would before long be an established actress, who mentioned that television commercials were where the big breaks were likely to come. 'Try that *Canada Dry* audition next week,' she was advised. Linda, by now called Evans because it would look better on the credits and be easier for potential producers to remember, tried the audition and got the job.

'All you've got to do,' advised the director, 'is drink the ginger ale and smile.'

It was a gift to a pretty young girl and she accepted it with all the alacrity she might have extended to a package neatly tied up with pink ribbon.

She had one competitor for the 'role' in the minute-long advertisement – the same Carole Wells, who would have her own big break before long in the *National Velvet* television series.

Linda beat her and seems to have enjoyed the experience. 'It was scarcely a dramatic *tour de force*,' she said.

The scene was a teenage party, boys in suits with narrow lapels and still narrower ties; girls with hair in pony tails and flouncing dirndle skirts. Linda played the hostess, all smiles and *sympatico*, serving Canada Dry to her guests. Everyone involved seemed to have as much fun as she did herself.

As she said, 'I was so enthralled by everyone's excitement when I served the Canada Dry that I failed to notice my boy friend had brought me flowers. But when I poured him some Canada Dry too, our romance was saved.'

There would never be a shortage of boy friends for Miss Linda Evans. Or, it would seem, of jobs, which was far from the usual situation for young, budding actresses.

After soft drinks, it was hard rides, for she was advertising Volkswagen cars next. She did well by that – with more dollars flooding into her bank account than ever before. Linda was now the sole breadwinner of her family.

It wasn't a tough ride in front of the Volkswagen cameras either. Linda only had to work for a few hours in the pleasant wide, open scenery which VW insisted represented the perfect background for their vehicles. And since the 'Beetle' car itself never changed – it certainly didn't at that time – the commercial didn't change either. For those couple of hours work, Linda drew residual royalty payments for the following five years or more.

That, it might be thought, was what show business was all about. Actually, it wasn't. She dreamed of being a real actress playing real roles for which a commercial sponsor had absolutely no responsibility.

It didn't happen all at once. But Linda was never really out of work. The girl with the pretty home-spun smile and the neat little figure was ideal for the family situations that the makers of commercials loved so much.

Linda was the Campbells Soup girl; a girl who also wore

nylons by DuPont and who enjoyed eating Mars bars. It was clear that the manufacturers realised that having Linda's shapely legs in their sheer stockings would be good for business. And if a girl with that delightful figure could keep it while devouring plates of tomato soup, and then – horrors for the Weight Watchers – be seen to enjoy chocolate and caramel, then she was the one to have on your side.

She was still at school when she was offered her first real TV role – playing a teenager madly in love as only a teenager could be in love with an older man. The object of her very deep affections was a young man with a mass of black hair – and not the slightest suggestion of grey, real or embellished. His name was John Forsythe.

Later, Forsythe was to describe her as a somewhat gangling, tall kid when they worked together in what became *Bachelor Father*, which was shot at Universal Studios. He had discovered Linda in a hotel lobby and recommended her to the people – Bachelor Productions – who were going to make the new series.

Bachelor Father was to be very, very important to her.

It was a marvellous time for a girl who admitted she was infected with the fever that strikes many another teenager. She was star-struck. Above her bed were pictures of the heart throbs of the day. In the centre of them all, the eyes staring at her almost hypnotically, was a certain young Canadian-born actor named John Derek.

Doubtless, at the time, she also dreamed of the day when people might have *her* picture above their beds, and in all probability the TV stations sending out publicity pictures of the pretty young Linda *were* dispatching them to spotty little boys dreaming of their first loves.

Bachelor Father was a TV series in which the young Miss Evans looked best in a shirt and checked trousers – which, one supposes, got things just about right. The woman who, with Forsythe again at her side, would play her age and make a fortune at it twenty years later, was earning a very nice living indeed doing just that, playing her age.

A film called *Bachelor Father* had been made by MGM with Marion Davies and C. Aubrey Smith – mainly about an elderly father visiting his young family. Plainly, this new series had little bearing on the original, made more than thirty years earlier.

She was then put under contract to MGM. The very initials still had a magic about them. To some people, they stood for Makers of Great Musicals. To others, they symbolised the stylish days of Hollywood, when girls in long white dresses stood in long white rooms, around the long lids of long grand pianos.

Other T V series followed, parts as teenagers in *The Adventures of Ozzie and Harriet* and the 1920s gangster series *The Untouchables*.

But not everything was exactly perfect for her.

2

It was a difficult time for Linda – and just how difficult would take years to be revealed.

She still kept remembering the trust her father had placed in her. In 1983, she recalled that her main aim in life was 'I didn't want to let him down.' But she was susceptible. And susceptible in the oldest way known to man – if not always to woman. Certainly not always to teenage girls, particularly those named Linda Evans.

Linda had gone out with a worker at a fairground – the kind of place with which she would be closely identified very soon – and she had lost her virginity to him.

As the result of one steamy session together, she had become pregnant, while still in her teens.

She liked men whom the tabloids would describe as beefcake. As to so many other seemingly prim, proper and shy young girls, men with oily overalls covering hard muscles had a fatal attraction.

In this case, the muscular one got Linda drunk, and made love to her behind a truck. It was not the kind of thing she would have liked her *Dynasty* fans to know about. At least that is how Patrick Curtis, who became her boy friend soon after that incident, was to tell it.

He said he discovered this was the reason Linda seemed so cold on their first dates together. She refused him anything more than a goodnight kiss – which in the 1950s wasn't altogether an unusual thing to happen. Most nice, well-brought up girls did draw the line at anything very much more than a kiss and a little petting.

Curtis was a budding film actor, who was working with her on *The Adventures of Ozzie and Harriet.*

Before long, they too, were lovers. But for the moment, she was playing very coy. It was only when he heard the sound of sobbing coming from her bedroom that he realised something was wrong. Curtis had taken her home and was already on his way out, when he heard the crying and the truth dawned. Soon, they were talking about the horror of it all.

She couldn't have the child. She wouldn't have the child. But what could they do? Linda was seventeen.

It was the twenty-year-old Curtis who suggested Mexico. He had been told that abortion was legal there.

Curtis drove her to Tijuana – only to be turned back by border police because she was under twenty-one. So he drove back into the United States, where Linda got out from the seat next to him and climbed into the trunk at the back. And that was how the two-months-pregnant Linda was taken into Mexico to have her forced miscarriage.

That, too, would prove to be something of an irony a quarter of a century later when the elegant matron would say that a child was the only real happiness missing from her life.

Curtis did his own best to compensate for anything else she was lacking. They were at the start of a very hot young love affair. The girl who to him had been the cute little starlet, became, as he was to describe her, a wild passionate woman.

It started soon after the abortion.

As they sat in the back of Curtis's car, on plastic covers made with different activities in mind by the young actor's grandmother, everything seemed to change. Impetuously, they began tearing at each other's clothing. Half naked, they made love there and then.

'We just got carried away,' recalled Curtis.

Later at a party, Linda told him they had to get engaged. Just like that. In fact, she said, if she weren't engaged by that coming Christmas, their love affair would be over.

Curtis was not convinced that Linda actually wanted to marry him. But like many another young girl she did want a wedding. Or at least an engagement.

So, Curtis says, he threw a party. And during it, he stood up on a chair and announced the coming nuptials to his guests who, naturally enough, started screaming, clapping and hugging the two of them.

It was a strange engagement – for what was turning out to be a fairly strange relationship. It couldn't be much else when the bride didn't really want to go to the altar and certainly not to take on all the responsibilities which would follow.

As he told it to writer Ruth Brotherhood, instead of a ring, he gave her a mongrel dog, half-spaniel, half-poodle, which they called a cockapoo.

They made love frequently, one night when both of them were turned on by a blue movie which Linda had said she wanted to see and which Curtis had tracked down with some considerable effort.

Together, they imitated – although the result was no imitation – everything being projected on to the wall behind them in Mrs Evanstad's apartment.

Their most popular haunt was the hallway in the flat. He said that only worked because Linda was so thin.

It was one of the times when her mother was trying to remedy, as she saw it, her husband's previous laxity. She was not allowing Linda to stay out late at night. So this mad, passionate love-making all took place during the day. If Mrs Evanstad or one of Linda's sisters arrived unexpectedly, there was a need for a hurried replacement of trousers, skirts, brassières and everything else that stood between what they were doing and outward respectability.

The affair was short-lived. Linda became attracted by another man – not the sort that Curtis said he liked – and before long they were to separate. Linda went her own way and Patrick his. Eventually he would marry Racquel Welch.

With the problem of pregnancy out of the way and having decided that Mr Curtis was not for her, Linda decided to concentrate more on her career.

Linda was enjoying being one of the last vestiges of the studio contract system. Besides anything, there was the chance of being at something of a screen finishing school. When she went to MGM in 1961, there were friendships to be made and friendships that would last. Among those with whom she became very friendly at the time was the young man starring in the *Dr Kildare* series, Richard Chamberlain.

She would spend the next twenty years denying that there was anything romantic about their relationship. 'We're just good friends,' she insisted, meant just that – and no more.

Work was hard, if not quite as hard as in the days when Louis B. Mayer himself instructed his people to dispense 'uppers' and 'downers' to Judy Garland.

Television executives thought they could spot talent when they saw it. That was why they decided she was the one they wanted for a new series called *Buttons*. They shot a pilot, built entirely around the feisty and busty young Linda.

The sponsors and the television networks were less impressed though.

It was literally a pilot which failed to take off and the cans of film gathered dust on the shelves in the vaults.

However, they did give her a role as an hysterical teenager in *The Eleventh Hour*. For the first time, Linda herself was singled out by critics who thought they saw the germ of an acting talent in the young beauty.

But it was that young beauty that MGM wanted to keep. They made her look cute and coy. Her hairstyle was short – they even allowed the blonde to get a little darker. Once more, someone saw the advantage her long legs brought to her career; legs which began at the floor and seemed to finish somewhere around her shoulders. So she was posed in floral baby-doll smocks, with floral baby-doll smiles to go with them.

Despite those legs, after two years, in 1963, MGM dropped her contract.

The following year, however, things began to look up. It was midsummer when three producers called on the now almost despondent Miss Evans.

Arthur Gardner, Jules Levy and Arnold Laven were about to go to Mexico to make yet another film about the war between the United States Cavalry and the Indians.

The film was to be called *The Glory Guys*. Would Linda be interested in playing the part of one of the glory guys' glory girls? She would wear lots of figure-hugging clothes that stood the risk of tearing in all but the most strategic places. Her face might get a little dirty, her hair unkempt, but they would guarantee to keep her looking beautiful.

How could she refuse? She couldn't. But she wouldn't make the film. The producers also interviewed Senta Berger and decided they liked the way she looked in those torn, figure-hugging dresses better, and so gave her the part.

Linda was offered a consolation prize. *The Glory Guys* was to be a big-budget bows-and-arrows, pistols-and-horses movie and she had hoped it would give her a chance to be noticed. The consolation prize was a T V series which would do rather more than that for her.

But it would take just a little while longer. Also, before very long, her personal life would change drastically. Soon there would be a man waiting for her with promises of support and guidance whose attentions would make Svengali seem like a benign, elderly gentleman with a heart of gold. But not just yet. First there was work to attend to.

Linda figured she needed a chance to do more with her career than she had yet achieved. And she was right. True, she was barely out of her teens, but it was a young people's business, a rat-race in which you were liable to be retired if you hadn't made it big by the time you were old enough even to carry a driver's licence.

And Linda had *not* yet made it big. A film she made early in 1964 called *Twilight of Honor* did nothing for either her or the few people who paid money at the box office to see it. But she did appear in it with Richard Chamberlain.

It was the story of a murder trial in a small American town. But it was Chamberlain's film and the best supporting role came from Claude Rains.

Then there was *Those Calloways*, made for Walt Disney about the efforts of a family busily engaged in protecting the flock of wild geese who had set up home close to their own cabin in the marshes of Maine.

This wasn't a Linda Evans spectacle either, although it had considerable charm and enabled Walter Brennan, Vera Miles and Brian Keith to play the sort of roles for which they were well suited and for Ed Wynn, one of the most lovable characters ever to graduate from Broadway vaudeville to Hollywood, to enjoy himself thoroughly.

One caught occasional glimpses of Linda, but not a great deal more.

At last the role she was being offered was not one to be easily rejected – not by a young girl whose ambition was at least as strong as her desire to look beautiful.

Linda would play Barbara Stanwyck's daughter in what the people at ABC television said would be a hugely important new T V series about a travelling carnival. There would be lots of well-built strong men in blue jeans and matching waistcoats. Linda would be allowed to grow her hair long and wear frilly blouses that wouldn't look out of place even when she was surrounded by bales of hay.

It had to seem like a good idea to both her and the various people who were now beginning to manage her career. The series would be called *The Big Valley* and looked set to be the biggest thing since Ben Cartwright and his sons set out for the Pondarosa in *Bonanza*. All the predictions seemed to indicate that *The Big Valley* would be a bonanza itself and with Linda having the second most important role in the series – second, in fact, only to Miss Stanwyck.

She would have been a fool to say no. And a fool she was not. But she had already accepted an offer of a big screen movie which was of a more doubtful nature.

Had Linda been a more important actress, the sensible thing would have been to decline and wait to make her name in *The Big Valley*. But at the age of twenty-three, there didn't seem a great deal to lose in accepting a role opposite Frankie Avalon, the hip-swinging pop-hero of 1965, in a movie called *Beach Blanket Bingo*.

If the title doesn't give an instant impression of cinematographic art, then at least it is no more than honest.

The now slightly plump Miss Evans was posed wearing a two-piece bathing costume (not a bikini) standing next to Mr Avalon and other young men in bathing shorts.

Before long, the title was changed to *Beach Party* and it would be the first of a whole string of banal pictures featuring young people in swimming attire who barely allowed themselves to get wet and spent most of their time innocently kissing and playing guitars. This one had a vague story about an anthropologist who was supposedly studying the habits of these insipid youngsters.

Robert Cummings, Dorothy Malone, Vincent Price, Morey Amsterdam (of the *Dick Van Dyke Show*) all competed for attention with the personable Mr Avalon. Linda wasn't even mentioned in the film's publicity.

The Big Valley would prove to do her a better service.

She was told to slim down, grow her hair, allow it to get more blonde, and be more of an innocent in the hard, tough world around her. And it worked.

She liked the series and, as far as anyone at ABC could tell, the audiences liked her too. New episodes were being churned out every week, and Linda seemed to thrive on it all.

By now she had a steady boyfriend. His name was Paul Raffles, and owned a nightclub called *PJs*. Like many another young, successful nightclub owner, he was as ambitious for the women in his life as he was for himself. It was Raffles who decided that Linda needed a public image for herself – if only to prevent her from sinking without trace in all the publicity hype for *The Big Valley*, the way she had in *Beach Party*.

He retained a public relations specialist for her.

Jay Bernstein was a man who many years later would have a very big effect on Linda's career, but for the moment he was instructed to provide Miss Evans with the kind of reputation which would make editors and photographers instantly glad that she had crossed their paths.

Bernstein, one of the whizzes of this tough business, accepted the challenge. He could see that Linda was an attractive girl who would look good in a hundred magazine spreads. Besides anything, he knew a great deal about *The Big Valley*. He also represented one of Linda's co-stars in the series, Peter Breek.

He had her photographed in the right places – which generally meant at the right parties – and placed little notices about the things that happened to her on the set of *The Big Valley* in all the Hollywood columns that counted. This was very important because it meant that even when the general public were not necessarily going to be terribly interested, the professionals – the producers and the agents – would be. And he made sure that she always looked as young and as fresh as she did on screen.

'The trouble was,' Bernstein told me, 'she hated doing publicity. She was basically very shy and really wasn't interested in creating any kind of public exposure.'

As he added: 'When the time was over, I think we were both happy. She wasn't easy. Always nice and ladylike. But she didn't like having a spotlight put on her. She wouldn't do interviews.' The relationship came to an end.

There was one other contributory factor. Linda had stopped going out with Raffles. She had met the man into whose eyes she confessed to have been staring since she was a teenager – John Derek.

3

Ironically, it had been Derek who had tried to make Bernstein's life a little easier. He had turned from acting to photography and had come on to *The Big Valley* set to take pictures of Linda. The pictures were taken and he, it appeared, had faded from her life.

Now, though, his role was totally different. When he met her again, he had more in mind for her than merely posing for his camera. And she was totally ensnared.

Derek represented glamour, security, love, admiration and – as Freudian students will easily recognise – a father figure, the kind of man she had been without since she was fifteen.

He had been thirty-eight when they first met – sixteen years older than her. They didn't see each other again for another two years. This time, he told her his marriage was in trouble. 'Funny thing,' she said, 'so is my engagement.' Which wasn't strictly true.

John Derek was an actor who had realised that he would never reach the kind of super-stardom that would have satisfied him. So be became an artist, a superb photographer, a some-time film producer, and considered himself a creator of women. The marriage which was in trouble was to Ursula Andress (the way *she* posed for pictures made one wonder whether it would have been more suitable to spell her surname with a 'U' instead of an 'A').

He had moulded Ursula the way Roger Vadim moulded Brigitte Bardot, Catherine Deneuve and Jane Fonda. As the years moved on, the similarity became more and more apparent.

Derek was born Derek Haris in 1926. By the time his first film *I'll Be Seeing You* went before the cameras, he was blessed with the kind of good looks that bordered on being pretty. His eyes – those eyes into which Linda Evans had gazed for so long from her bed – were dark. So was his hair.

In films like *Knock On Any Door*, *All The King's Men* and *Prince of Players* (a picture about Edwin Booth – the actor who murdered Abraham Lincoln – starring Richard Burton), Derek showed a degree of talent which for a time caused a great deal of excitement. Not least among the many girls who courted his attention.

They saw in him a sex symbol – and perhaps also a creator of sex symbols. If he could do for them what he had done for Ursula Andress, the star of *Dr No*, *She* and most recently, in 1965, *What's New Pussycat*, then he was the man to know.

And equally clearly, Derek loved being with women as much as he enjoyed shaping their careers.

Now, in 1965, he was directing *Once Before I Die*, a picture in which he was also co-starring – with Ursula.

It was just the time their marriage was crashing against the rocks that had destroyed so many other Hollywood loves. His daughter by his first marriage, Sean, was living also with him. She was to share the suffering of many other children from broken homes.

The movie was about US troops in the Philippines during World War Two, but to Linda, the story mattered not one bit.

She was plainly bowled over by Mr Derek, just like all those other girls. And Derek was equally struck by Linda. He took her for dinner and they became lovers. When his marriage finally ended in divorce, there was no doubt that Linda was ready to step into Ursula's place and take over her bed.

In fact Ursula had been the first to leave. She had fallen for the French actor Jean-Paul Belmondo, who at the time was rather more successful and perhaps more sexy than Mr Derek. John and Linda lived together.

Relations between Ursula and Linda were at first – predictably – tense.

The new woman on the John Derek scene was highly disturbed by the lingering influence of the older one. From the home she had set up with M. Belmondo, Ursula would write loving and sexy letters to the man who was still officially her husband.

His birthday would be marked by a card, equally loving, from Ursula while Linda was the one in his home. Then there would be other cards – like 'Happy anniversary, darling.'

As Linda noted subsequently: 'I would think, "Happy anniversary!" And she's not even with him – I am! What *is* this?" '

What this *was* was the fury of a woman in love with a man who apparently had been scorned – the like of which hell hath no fury, for all that is said about the rejected woman.

Well-meaning friends – Linda herself thought them otherwise – warned her of the ubiquitous Ursula: she would keep her well-manicured claws into the man Linda loved and hoped eventually to marry.

Even John's closest associates – and there were not many of those – brought her the same, familiar warnings: 'Ursula and John will get together again. They loved each other too much to part now. This is only a temporary split.'

None of that was particularly encouraging to Linda who would hear the name Ursula Andress and go quietly berserk.

But things were to change, and quite quickly. For one day, Linda and Ursula met – on the doorstep of the Beverly Hills house which Linda now considered home and which Ursula had always believed was hers, too.

Suddenly, the fear and the hatred changed. Indeed, they both melted.

Simply what happened was that Ursula knocked on the door and Linda went to answer it. This was a situation with which many a suburban housewife has been faced. In the Hollywood community, where lawyers seem to be brought in to write notes for the neighbourhood milkman, it is considerably rarer.

Quite suddenly, Linda was meeting the woman who was still legally married to her own lover.

She was to say that the two women just 'sort of looked at each other'. If that scene had been re-enacted by one of the comic papers telling the stories of Hollywood people, a series of daggers would have been indicated travelling between their eyes.

All Ursula said, in a tiny thin voice, was: 'Is John home?' She wasn't interested in making polite conversation. How could she, after all? To Linda it seemed that being polite was a state of mind that wasn't going to be uppermost in her predecessor's intent. Except she was wrong. . . .

The two women had more in common than they could possibly have imagined. For one thing, Ursula was painfully shy, extraordinarily nervous.

And it all came bubbling out through the silence of the meeting that day.

Ursula was as pained and as emotional as Linda. She took one look at the new occupant and burst into tears.

Linda stared at her, at this woman who in the movies had seemed so strong and powerful, who had appeared to be so domineering, and yet who now looked like a tiny waif. That look was enough: 'How am I supposed to hate this person?' she asked herself. And decided not to do so. From that moment on, if Linda's version of the story is to be believed, they became firm friends.

Quite clearly, it took more than that. But become friends they did – and good friends, too.

As for Ursula's effect on her own relationship with John, Linda had no need to worry. Two years after first getting together, she and John were married.

He started framing her career. It was Derek who was representing her as a publicist. If anyone was going to organise Linda Evans's career it was going to be Mr Derek.

He was going to make her a superstar, just as he almost had with Ursula. At least, he was going to ensure that she was a young woman people would remember.

For one thing, Derek wasn't all that impressed with *The Big Valley*.

He did not believe that playing Barbara Stanwyck's daughter Audra Barkley did enough for her. She was a well-established TV personality, but that wasn't enough. Stanwyck was the star of the piece. Derek believed it should be Linda.

Linda herself wasn't quite so keen about dropping out of the series. She went on to do 112 episodes, but all the time Derek was desperate to take her away from the bales of straw.

And he had a point, as Linda herself was to admit, 'All I did was ride a horse a little bit each week.'

There was a more sophisticated Linda inside that bosom-hugging blouse and he was determined to get her out. It was he who supervised her hairstyle, who sought out the right make-up artists, who got her to look precisely the way he wanted her.

Was he really a Svengali? In as much as Linda was a willing Trilby, exacting from him quite as much as he was taking from her, there can be no doubt. When he was around, she functioned in the new image that he was tailoring for her in no less a detailed way than the dressmakers he personally supervised were fashioning her wardrobe.

At twenty-three years of age, Linda Evans was perhaps more a new kind of Eliza Doolittle in a totally different *Pygmalion*.

Just before he married Linda, in a last desperate attempt at keeping things going with Ursula, Derek had photographed his wife for a twelve-page spread in *Playboy*.

In those twelve pages, she really was Ursula Undress. Linda wasn't ready for that yet, although it *was* the kind of exposure John was convinced was necessary to get her talked about. Couple that belief with his own decision to fire a professional public relations adviser and you see something of the confusion this already fairly confused young lady was having to put up with.

One thing that didn't faze her was John's daughter, Sean. They developed a lasting relationship which would cause more than a few problems in the *Dynasty* era, but for the moment,

Linda had found a new home and a new family as well as a new man in her life.

It was a happy development, putting aside the morals of taking over another woman's place. A girl still so pitifully insecure as Linda undoubtedly needed the sort of pushes that John was administering and she showed both the need and the appreciation.

Even if she had been tough enough to withstand the pressures and demands of producers who were more out to make a fast buck with a girl who made ideal camera fodder, rather than quality movies, she still needed a strong influence to back her up.

John Derek was that all right, from the moment she moved into his life. 'I encouraged him to do everything for me,' she was to accept.

He not only decided her clothes and personal appearance, he told her what to eat – some of those early TV shots, to say nothing of the way she looked in *Beach Party* – show a girl who was not just well rounded in the places girls were supposed to be rounded, but one with a certain amount of what used to be politely called puppy fat.

She wasn't the same girl Patrick Curtis knew – in appearance or personality.

Derek watched her figure from a professional as well as a human, masculine point of view. He had a hunch that those curves could be a passport to an important career as well as to a satisfying sexual relationship.

But she was still totally insecure. Getting to the top was as difficult as ever. With no *Big Valley* to work on, she could have hoped that the new lifestyle was going to open the big new doors she was waiting for. It didn't happen – and she felt no more secure for that. Except that now she was once more playing one of her 'Let's pretend' games, and this time she was pretending that it didn't matter. 'My personal life is more important,' she would say.

There were no big film offers that Derek thought suitable. No television series that would make her the Big Star, even if not the Super Star. (There were no Mega Stars just yet.) Before long, they were planning the film they would make together, but it would take time – a very long time – to get off the ground.

It was fortunate that she did have a satisfying personal life. Had Linda been at her family's North Hollywood home, she would have had to start playing those old games – with her mother now as the central object. Mrs Evanstad was seriously ill and was spending much of her time in bed. Had she still been there, the old sensitivity might have become intolerable for her.

She was grateful for what John Derek brought her. He was to say perhaps a little too grateful, a little too much clinging to what others took very much for granted. As he once said: 'I used to walk into the room and Linda would light up like a Christmas tree. Then one day I realised that when *anyone* walked into the room, Linda lit up like a Christmas tree. When the friggin' maid walked into the room for Christ's sake.'

All the same, it wasn't an easy, simple life for the young Mrs Derek.

She began looking into religion – all religions. She sampled them all, almost as though she were choosing a new belief by mail order.

Meditation was what she liked best, which was why for a time the Eastern religions were the ones that appealed most.

'I began to seek my own way of honouring God in my life,' she was to confess. 'I myself don't believe you have to go to church to have a talk with God. How you walk through life is how you honour God.'

Perhaps she would have liked to have honoured Him by having a child? She would have done, but Derek wasn't quite so keen. It might have interrupted that career, and even more important, spoilt that figure.

There were the compensations of their own love together. And she was getting to know and even to love John's daughter Sean.

Somehow, she felt she knew Sean even before they began a series of long, detailed meetings together. Sean wrote her father

Early publicity pictures of
the starlet Linda Evans.

ABC-TV's *The Big Valley*, starring (*left to right*) Lee Majors, Peter Breck, Linda Evans, Richard Long and Barbara Stanwyck (1965).

Mitchell (1974) in which Linda co-starred with the tough young American Joe Don Baker.

As an American agent in the TV film *Avalanche Express*, Linda was the only female star.

In *Tom Horn* (1980) Linda played a headstrong schoolteacher opposite Steve McQueen (*below*).

Linda attends the Annual People's Choice Awards in 1983 with society restaurateur George San Pietro.

Linda cherished the relationship with her *Dynasty* husband, oil tycoon Blake Carrington played by John Forsythe.

In January 1981 the compelling new
television series *Dynasty* was all set to
rival *Dallas*.

John and Bo Derek in 1981.

regular letters and Linda read them all. 'I cared about Sean from the first moment I saw her. I felt that I understood her. I saw her love.' Which Sean would later suggest was more than her father himself did. 'I was quite fond of her even before I knew her,' Linda recalled.

Before long, Sean came to live with her father and his new wife, who quite plainly wasn't at all the conventional idea of a stepmother.

John, she said, was proud to have her back with him. Even excited.

Linda could see that, even though that emotion wasn't particularly evident in everything he did or said. As she was to say: 'I saw how much John seemed to need this relationship with her. I've always felt that John does love – even though he has a very unusual way of expressing it.'

As far as Sean was concerned, Linda was her 'Little Mommy'.

Not so to Sean's elder brother, Russell, or Russ, who was showing many of the symptoms of a child from a broken home.

He had already a record of juvenile delinquency. He wasn't quite the sort of youngster Linda liked being around. She would later admit that she didn't really trust him. 'He was always rather difficult and he didn't allow you to get close to him.' (Later, Russ would be involved in a motor-cycle accident and become a quadraplegic).

Linda still had the friends she had made in her previous existence – which, considering the appeal of the Eastern religions, might have been the way she chose to look at all that had gone before.

She and Barbara Stanwyck stayed on good terms, and that says a lot for the way *The Big Valley* had been run. In not a few cases, people acting out close relationships – especially women – tend to develop almost neurotic resentments, if not hates.

Ever since the TV series, Linda has sent Barbara a bouquet every Mother's Day.

But most of the time was spent with John, and John seemed to like it that way as much as she did.

33

'John is a loner,' Linda would say, and people who considered themselves friends and were suddenly excluded from their company had to resign themselves to that fact.

So did Linda. 'He likes to be away from everyone. I am a people person,' she would say.

But the nagging fact that as an actress – let alone as a star – she was on a hiding to nothing grew more and more pressing. And with it the insecurity.

John wanted her to look pretty and to stay looking pretty. To her, it wasn't enough, but there was just nothing she could do about it. He was the one who called the shots and she had to obey his bidding. There was no spell cast on her, but the way she behaved made it seem that way.

The other reason she didn't get parts was they never saw anyone for weeks on end. 'He's very anti-social,' Linda was to say about John. Yet friends who did meet them at the occasional parties they attended recall that John was much, much more outgoing than his wife, who looked beautiful, laughed at his jokes but made very little conversation.

For a long time, she was attempting to say clearly that she really wanted nothing more. 'It was the most wonderful life I can imagine any woman having,' she recalled for *People* magazine in 1980.

When she was out on one of the few filming engagements she did manage to land, Derek would greet her return with an embrace that would have looked sensational had they done it before a wide-screen camera.

There was champagne waiting in a silver bucket, and next to it a salver with grapes which she insisted were individually dusted with sugar – in case they were slightly sour. And it was all laid out on a bed of fur which he prepared by the fireplace. It always seemed a pity that it wasn't cold enough for an actual fire. Even if it had been, he would have warmed her sufficiently with his ardour.

He himself made a pair of superbly decorated boots for her. When that was done, he switched his attention to a waistcoat, finely embroidered by the same Mr John Derek.

People knew about the way he seemed to manipulate his wife, refusing to allow her to wear certain shades of lipstick or nail varnish. Exploitation, they mumbled to themselves – few papers were interested in the happenings of Miss Evans at the time, so the mumbles stayed merely mumbles.

It wasn't manipulation, Linda insisted all along. 'He cares about beauty more than anyone I've ever known,' she maintained years later. 'He would have made a wonderful knight of the Round Table.' The mind boggles at the thought of Sir John in shiny armour armed with a lance ready to slay a dragon breathing fire over M'Lady Linda.

As for herself, she was beginning to feel something of a fraud. She may have trained to be a model, but apart from the drama class at school, she had had no acting lessons to speak of and now she was beginning to blame that lack of vocational education for the lack of success in her career.

'I wish I had more courage,' she told people, some of whom thought that being married to Mr Derek must have been a fairly courageous thing in itself – except that Mr Derek cared for her passionately and hoped that waiting for the right thing to come along was enough.

It soon became obvious, however, that by the time she had reached her twenties, she was practically retired. It was the age of the mini-skirt, but there were huge crowds of mini-skirted girls lining up at agents' offices for the kind of roles that had now passed Linda Evans by. And there was nothing on offer for girls closer to her age. Twenty-five was the perfect age, but some directors had come to the conclusion that Linda wasn't really a perfect actress – yet.

The main problem was that she was never really sure what her own role should be. She wanted to be just as pretty as Derek wanted her to be. She wanted to be feminine. As far as she was concerned, that meant being submissive – and in everything, not merely as part of the sexual act.

It was the way her mother had been and that was how she thought a woman should be. As Linda said: 'I always thought for a woman to be strong, she had to be overbearing. My mother ... would have been happier if she had been more assertive.'

And she added: 'I wanted to be helpless so that men would take care of me. I was good Little Linda. I didn't want to plan, speak, think.' Her inhibitions were very simple – based on the fact that she was just afraid of making the wrong decisions – about anything, anything at all.

She was playing it safe, and suffering from all the consequences that would come from doing just that.

Even so, she worked at being submissive – gave in to John's wiles even when perhaps she didn't want to do so. In her own words, she did her own bit of manipulating. And she agrees, she manipulated to be loved. The girl who had lost her real father at fifteen was already frightened she might now be losing another one.

Bunky Young, Linda's secretary, who knew her at that time, agrees that she was a 'pushover'. It was not a healthy thing for a young married woman to be.

But to Sean and Russ, Linda was a perfect helpmeet. 'She was a wonderful stepmother,' Sean has since recalled.

The house they had at Beverly Hills was very much a home, not one of the star-belt museums like the mansion in *Dynasty*.

She liked that and started insisting to everyone that she no longer minded *at all* not working. 'John wants nothing more than for his wife to be at home with him, or travelling with him, or doing whatever *he's* doing.'

They travelled to Europe together, set up homes overseas. And John photographed her everywhere – sometimes, in fact frequently, in the nude. Did nude pictures really conform with the image she wanted of being a lady?

'Very few people can shoot a woman without her clothes and have her look as good as John can,' she explained. And then added: 'They were just for the two of us.'

Not quite. Some of them appeared in *Playboy* in July 1971 – in which a flaxen-haired beauty, with a piece of rope hanging from her ear and crown, with a string bow around her neck swam among the bullrushes and looked beautiful.

She looked more than that. She looked both simple and ravishing. Her breasts were shown to be firm with pert, pointed nipples. Her face had a slightly far-away little-girl look. The enticing thing about these photographs – knowing what was to happen one day – is that if one were to caption them 'Bo Derek' instead of 'Linda Evans', there would be few who would venture to correct them.

Commenting about the quality of the pictures, the *Playboy* caption writer noted that they were the work of Linda's husband, and conceded: 'She's a lensman's dream, and he's clearly one who knows a perfect vision when he sees her.'

As John himself said: 'Linda is absolutely natural and uninhibited [Never quite true, particularly at this stage of her life] with or without clothing. So often a woman tries to act seductive during a nude shooting, usually because she must overcome a fear of being photographed unclad. But then the finished picture strikes you as fake. That's never the result when I photograph Linda. She's completely at ease and doesn't have to fear the camera, because physically she's in extraordinary shape.'

There could be no inhibitions about admitting that. She wasn't well enough known for *Playboy* to take an interest in a Linda Evans nude portfolio if she hadn't been – and there were as many beautiful girls standing in line to be photographed (at the time for $1,000 a go) without their clothes for a centrefold as there were hoping to be discovered for a Hollywood film. To many of them, of course, the chance of being featured in *Playboy* was an important step on the way to that discovery. The fact that few were, had little relevance to the queues lining up for the magazine's editor-in-chief, Hugh Hefner.

Linda was now twenty-seven years old.

But why would she permit those pictures to be published? She would always insist that she didn't know they were going to be offered either to *Playboy* or to anyone else. As she said, she thought they were intended for just the two of them.

Nevertheless, as she would say in another context years

later: 'When you're with John, he's always taking *millions* of pictures of you.'

However, there was a motive in the publication – apart from the fact that it was very good publicity for John Derek as a photographer: the soft focus, almost linen look of some of the pictures showed him to be very much an artist with his lens – he and Linda had finally made a movie together. *Wildflowers* was the summit of their professional ambitions together, the picture she said she had been waiting for before resuming her professional career.

Alas, it was wishful thinking. Since no one remembered hearing of Linda Evans – even though *The Big Valley* was still playing on local television stations throughout America (as it still is in some places) – Derek needed all the publicity he could get. And those pictures were that all right. Unfortunately, they were not enough.

The movie, written, produced and directed by John featuring his nude wife (1971 was the year when most films managed to feature a nude scene) was so bad that it couldn't even get itself a release; a fact for which Linda has subsequently had good reason to be grateful.

Linda insisted that it was 'something more than a puppet part.' That was in distinct contrast to the sort of roles that were being offered to her. 'I'm afraid most of the roles seem stereotyped and just plain dull. Besides, I don't feel the need any more to prove that I'm an actress.'

That was not true then, and it would not be true for several years to come. The fact that she felt the need to say it spoke volumes.

There were people knocking on her door now, however, either because they *had* heard of *Wildflowers* or perhaps – and more likely – they had not.

She was being offered a number of TV parts. But she said she wasn't interested. 'There's nothing exciting me.'

Unfortunately for Linda, the more likely case was that there was nothing to excite John Derek. He wanted her to do work of which he approved and perhaps he still wanted to do more with her in front of the cameras. But there would be no other *Wildflowers*.

There was also an additional sadness in her life. That year, when Linda was twenty-nine, her mother died. Once more, she tried to pretend that it hadn't happened, but the reaction wasn't as strong as when her father died and before very long she was able to come more to terms with the situation, both situations.

She was grateful enough for the way John conducted himself during those years of married life. 'John is a very honorable man,' she was to say. 'When he flirts with you, he never looks at or flirts with anybody else. You don't have to be nervous, you don't have to worry about protecting yourself.'

They were words that would be eaten and with a considerable pinch of salt.

One thing that he was helping her to achieve was the art of growing up.

It was a different kind of marriage than the sort she had dreamed of when she was a little girl. 'As a child,' she was to recall, 'I dreamed of getting married, having a flower garden and having children.'

There was a flower garden ready made for her at Derek's Beverly Hills house. But no children. It depressed her. Being without children when they want them depresses most women. But nobody knew about her longing. Those who did know her seemed to assume that it was either a mutual choice or John's alone.

Mr Derek, whose hair was now grey and long, but whose eyes were as strong and dark as ever, wasn't likely to talk about it. It is also certain that if he had decided there would be no children, no children there would be.

Despite the obvious control that John exerted on her life, she was living much of it the way that she wanted. It was as an informal girl, managing to carry on an extremely informal life. No elegantly dressed servants in their house. No mink coats to wear for film premières.

Her favourite clothes were a pair of boots over her jeans and a silk blouse on top. 'Real clothes,' as she put it, held no interest for her at all.

But what about that career? If John wasn't around to dictate her next move, would she really have abandoned it all – and at such an early age?

She protested that nothing mattered, even though her last film wasn't seen by anyone apart from those *Playboy* readers.

'I never planned to be an actress,' she said, quite some time afterwards and, in truth, behaving like many another actress telling a story which totally contradicted the one she had told before (and several times, too.) 'I'm not competitive and find it interesting that a career has come so easily to me. I also feel very blessed that I've been able to do as much as I have, but my personal life has always been most important to me.'

That she had said before. But now she was adding: 'I can't see myself living out my old age with my awards.'

So there had to be more to her life. Her search for God continued. She decided to study French as well as metaphysics. She was learning to play tennis and was enjoying as much of the game as she could get in. Even John Derek, who believed in his own style of perfection, had to admit that she was a very good cook.

'I found it impossible not to fall in love with him,' she said about John. And that was how it seemed to be continuing. The grapes were always there waiting for her, sometimes individually dipped in eggwhite before being coated with the sugar.

Every time that Linda mentioned she might want to go back to work, it was Derek who stopped her even considering it. He all but handed her an ultimatum: 'Hollywood or me.'

For the moment, there was no reason to doubt that the situation would go on for ever and ever. She was his queen and was installed on a throne of his making, even if it was in the shape of a fur rug.

As far as she was concerned, the house – wherever it was situated, was Mount Olympus and John Derek was her own personal god.

'He wants to work with you and be with you twenty-four hours a day,' she said. 'He's constantly pushing you to improve.'

That love was being expressed in the ways in which she had come to expect it to be expressed. He bought special parchment paper – so that he could write long love poems to her.

Sometimes, the paper was a foot long and filled with odes to Linda's beauty and the love he felt for her. She showed *her* love in different, more obvious ways. Writing poetry wasn't up her particular part of the street. But she enjoyed receiving it.

For her, a love poem was the way she embraced John, the way she comforted him, how she told him she worshipped him. Sometimes, her poetry came in the dishes she created for him.

Since there were still no more attractive offers of work, it wasn't a hard ultimatum to accept and abide by.

And it was a situation that hardly changed until ten years after their first affair and eight years after their wedding. . . .

In 1973, John went to Greece to make a new film he was directing.

It was called *Once Upon A Time* and, just as in the fairy stories with which those words usually begin, it was to lead to very much more.

Linda left him to it and was happy to join him on location a couple of months later. By then, however, he had taken an interest in the film's sixteen-year-old *ingénue* which was not entirely professional.

Mary Cathleen Collins wasn't a marvellous actress, but had a pretty face which looked so much like Linda's and a thrilling figure which wasn't unlike hers either.

Derek had given Mary Cathleen a new name. He called her 'Bo'. What Linda called her isn't on the record. She did, however, admit soon afterwards that she wanted to kill them both.

Linda said she had seen it coming, watching the two working – and playing – together.

'I saw it happening. It wasn't planned by either of them, but

I could see John falling in love with Bo, while we were filming in Greece.'

So Linda left them to it.

She was, she has since said, 'sensing that John was determined to have the relationship. I thought that if I stayed it would only push him away from me.'

But he was being pushed away from her – and in public, too.

It was as hard for Linda as one would imagine. 'I can't describe what it's like to arrive on location weeks later and be told by a man you had shared everything with for almost ten years that he still loves you, but that he's also in love with someone else.'

Particularly hard since it was Linda herself who had introduced her to John. She had noticed Bo as a teenage actress and thought John might make use of her in his new film. Just what use he would put her to she could not even have imagined.

Bo – adopting the stance of 'Let's-all-Love Everybody', which would be adopted by Linda herself almost immediately afterwards – was to say that her predecessor took it all like an angel.

Linda, in an uncharacteristic tough mood, said: 'I don't remember being angelic.' Indeed, she would have been less of a normal woman and more of a super-human if she *had* greeted it as just one of those things and kissed the other two parties on the cheek, patted their heads and wished them luck.

John told her he had fallen in love with the ever-smiling and apparently simpering Bo and that they would have to divorce.

'I remember,' Linda was to recall, 'some yelling and screaming on my part and being very hurt. But if that's the way Bo prefers to remember it, that's all right, too.'

She didn't give that impression at the time – and nobody should have expected her to do so. 'I was hurt, jealous, angry, resentful - all the normal emotions. I longed to have and to keep what I wanted and considered mine.'

Miss Andress might have felt the same sort of thing when

she saw Linda in her house, but Ursula after all, had taken the first step.

When John told Linda that his mind was finally made up, she had the choice of either accepting the unpalatable truth or fighting it.

As she said: 'I had the option of hating them both and saying "You are unacceptable people and I never want to see you again" and in the process I would have become a bitter, unloving shrivelled-up woman.'

That wasn't what she tried to do at all. She said, like Bo – who was in a much better position to do so – 'Let's be friends.'

Certainly, on the outside anyway, Linda wasn't showing any huge resentment against the woman who had taken over her bed. But there was one thing for certain – her marriage was over. Yet it would have to end on her terms, not John's.

4

It was the end of a marriage and the end of a life style. The insecure Linda Evans had to take a decision on her own – for the first time since she and John Derek had first set up home together.

Either she had to sit and cry, or she had to decide that there was a future out there somewhere and that it had to be hers to grab where she could.

But at first she wasn't saying anything about the way she felt. Even John was frustrated about that. He once told a reporter: 'Tell Linda to get off her butt and tell you good things about me.' That was surprising. The one thing a husband leaving his wife doesn't expect her to say about him is good things. But this was different, he believed. Perhaps he also thought that his Svengali act would be strong enough to prevent her saying anything that was unpleasant.

The difficulty that Linda felt was that she was still very much in love with her husband, even when she was consulting lawyers about their divorce.

But Bo was casting the kind of shadows over her which Ursula had ten years before.

Certainly, she felt bitter, but if John had phoned her, sent her a bunch of flowers and found a way to secrete into her house a bottle of champagne and a collection of dusted grapes, she would have run into his arms.

'It was too sudden for me to deal with in any kind of rational way,' she was to admit eight years later. 'It was wonderful with John,' she agreed. 'But it could not have gone on for ever. It had to change. *I* had to change.'

What she was not changing was her love for him. It would continue.

So would the nagging fear over Bo, although here, too, she was recalling her relationship with the former Mrs Derek. Linda was now hoping for the sort of outcome John's friends – wrongly, as it turned out – had envisaged for Ursula Andress.

'I believed,' said Linda, 'if I gave him enough time, he would come to his senses, realise that it was impossible for him to stay with this child.' The word 'child' was biting and was intended as such.

'The last thing I wanted to do was to fall in love with someone else. I was sure John would come back.'

It was a hope enhanced by Derek's behaviour, once he had started to live with Bo. He started phoning Linda. He told her he still loved her. He said he still yearned for her company. But he made no mention of wanting to return to her or give up the 'child'.

As she would say, *he* sounded very, very confused.

But now *she* was going to try to chase that career. However, the more she tried to put her marriage behind her and think only of work, the more she had to admit she still loved the man who had been her husband.

Whether she would have loved him even more had he given her a child is a matter of conjecture. 'But that would have been impossible with John,' she would say, without giving any convincing reason. Spectators of the Derek marriage might have concluded that the reason was that a child could have complicated the kind of backwoodsman style that John liked to affect with his homespun waistcoats and personally-crafted boots.

John had certainly moulded her as a woman. The posture as she walked was the one he had dictated for her. The make-up was the kind he had said was right for her complexion. The clothes and the hair were the styles he had said were those he liked her to wear.

No change of marital status could alter this. She wasn't about to start cutting her hair differently or wearing anything he wouldn't previously have liked. The mark of Derek had been indelible.

Nor was Linda pretending anything different. Finally she was telling anyone who would listen – and now it seemed, the grief was too obvious to try to hide or for her to want to shield herself from other company – that she still loved John desperately. Yes, she was deeply hurt. Yes, she might even have meant it when she said she could have killed both John and the girl he was making in her image and calling Bo Derek.

But in the quieter moments, when the sobs had gone and the eyes dried, she said: 'The romance never stopped. It never does with John.'

And as if to prove it, she was going out of her way to say how much she liked Bo. And that went for Ursula, too. It was almost as though she were thinking of calling for the foundation of a Union of John Derek's Women. They all loved each other and they all loved John. He was the binding factor.

One didn't have to be too much of a cynic to cast doubt on that assertion. Yet, yet, yet . . . It really did look that way. What was more, she was staying very close to Sean and to her brother, Russ. When Russ was involved in his serious motor-cycle accident Linda forgot her inhibitions about him and she rushed round to give comfort, to offer to do whatever she possibly could for his mother, her predecessor-but-one as Mrs Derek.

There was another factor, too – one that Linda wouldn't admit to herself until many years afterwards. 'The fact that John and I split up when we did couldn't have been more perfect. When I was with John, a part of me was totally closed off. I needed to move on.'

Needing to and actually doing so were not necessarily the same thing. Yes, she had to think about that career, but agents weren't exactly knocking down her door to get her good parts. Being the former Mrs Derek was far from enough.

She had made a film starring Martin Balsam, John Saxon

and Joy Baker called *Mitchell*, a story about a drugs ring, but it had made no more impact than most of the other things she had been doing.

Her separation had received little coverage in the newspapers, not even so much as a stir among the delicatessens and coffee shops of Beverly Hills. It is here that the business part of show business meets to discuss the marital habits of the natives as though they were anthropologists wondering about the importation of a rare species of monkey.

It was that feature of the industry which so many actors and actresses disliked so much – Linda among them.

When she and John parted, a friend sent her a note: 'Congratulations, you've graduated from the John Derek School of Life'.

It was a good description, although now she felt she needed something in the way of a finishing school.

What she did need was to prove to herself as well as other people that she could survive in the big outside world, without John or anyone like him flattering her by his constant attention.

She *had* felt flattered by the care John displayed when she was around. But she had also begun to feel more than a little stifled by it. Once released from that crushing environment, could she make it on her own?

John was constantly with her mentally. Everything seemed to bring him back to her mind, even unrelated things like a pleasant day and a picturesque landscape. 'He is a true artist,' she would say. 'He cares more about beauty than anyone I've ever known. He taught me how to see beauty in life.'

Inevitably, she worried about withdrawal symptoms.

There were plenty of those all right – if only because she didn't have John to comment when that new dress was delivered. No longer would she wonder whether he would like the low neckline. He wasn't there any more when her hairdresser dictated the very slightest variation on the familiar style. Did she have the confidence to approve those changes on her own?

Her happiest moment at that time was when she told herself

she did have that confidence. She didn't need anyone at all to tell her whether her clothes or her appearance looked good.

And what was more, Linda liked it that way. She also discovered – and this was the big, big surprise – that she didn't mind being alone. She rather liked that independence, but this state didn't last for long.

Linda was invited now to parties, to openings, to those events at which the higher echelons of Los Angeles and Beverly Hills society preen themselves, the affairs – with a small 'a' – at the Beverly Hilton or the Beverly Wilshire. She was a valued customer at the first boutiques opening up on Rodeo Drive. And she was meeting wealthy, attractive men who asked her out.

Now she was realising that Linda Evans was herself something of a status symbol. She wasn't being asked because she was famous and well known – only those who bothered to know about her separation thought about that – but because she was a very pretty woman indeed, and one who could hold up a decent conversation.

Before long, there was one constant companion for Linda, a property millionaire named Stanley Herman, proprietor of Stanley Herman Realty, Inc. Even in Beverly Hills, they didn't come much more successful or richer than Mr Herman.

They met soon after Linda had flown back to Beverly Hills from Greece. The house in which the Dereks had lived would be hers, John agreed. So now it was hers to put on the market. Stan Herman was the first to come and look it over.

'Stan was warm and not at all pushy,' she remembered five years later. But that warmth, some might have called it suavity, was hot enough for their relationship to be more than just professional very early on. He found excuses to ring her up and to invite her for dinner.

He was six years older than Linda and from a totally different background both from her and John. There had been no pictures of Mr Herman pinned up above the juvenile Linda Evanstad's bed.

Divorced in 1959, he had been living what most people

considered to be a bachelor's life since then. He had dated some of the prettiest women in Hollywood, dressed impeccably, drove the best cars and was, all-in-all, considered one of the most eligible men in the vicinity.

That did not mean that he enjoyed life particularly. As he was to say, 'Ultimately, that kind of lifestyle gets very lonely.' Even with a beach-side home in Malibu which had once belonged to Laurence Harvey.

Linda, he decided soon after their first meeting, would look grand ensconced in the Malibu house.

He courted her with all the intensity a woman like Linda appreciated, the gifts, the flowers, the words that went with them. She was being wooed – and she liked it very much indeed.

It was very different from being with John. Somehow, she wasn't merely a Derek appendage, a doll that he was creating. She enjoyed being accepted and courted for herself. Suddenly, she wasn't the child she had, even now in her thirties felt herself to be.

There were still those who thought that John would come back. But when Linda accepted an invitation from Herman to spend two weeks with him in Tahiti, the talk died down.

She lived with him for two years before they agreed to marry. As Linda has since said, until then, she hadn't felt 'sure enough of the relationship to call John and ask for a divorce.'

But the call *was* eventually made.

No one was surprised when it leaked out that she had asked John for a divorce. When the decree came through – quite a year before John wed his Bo – she married Herman. It was 1976 when the ceremony took place and she moved into the Malibu house. And then very quickly moved out again. Stan had rented it out.

Someone wanted a house urgently and Mr Herman was anxious to oblige – and to pocket the $8,000 a week 'found money' he could charge.

Linda had to get used to his art of mixing business with pleasure – like selling a house at a party, answering real-estate calls in bed and deciding in the course of a short car journey to buy the home of silent movie star Harold Lloyd which was coming on to the market soon after his death – for $1,500,000. Linda was fast learning that sort of sum could be made to sound like chicken feed.

Herman had always been a man with determination. It had been exhibited when his first accountant examined his books and told him he was broke. So Stan took firm action – and fired the accountant. 'I can't stand negative thinking,' he explained. Neither would he accept it from Linda. She was going to be given only the best – and was under firm instructions to enjoy it whether she wanted to or not. With that kind of positive thinking in mind, there wasn't a lot she could do about it but comply. And start enjoying herself.

This was a new Linda Evans. As Mrs Herman, she was still struggling to find a professional image for herself, but her own self-esteem was never higher. Quite suddenly, as though she had been injected with a mystery serum, her personality had changed. She felt that she was Herman's equal. She had a mind of her own, and he was allowing her to express it.

On their first anniversary, Stan gave her a big party at the Malibu pad. Linda cooked the chicken, cheese soufflé and apple pie – helped by her friends Dani Janssen (wife of David Janssen, the TV actor best remembered for *The Fugitive*) and Alana Hamilton. Jack Hayley, his wife, Liza Minnelli, and Marisa Berenson were on hand, too.

The public were becoming interested in Linda – but not as a star or as an actress, simply as half of the fabulously wealthy Herman couple.

When they went shopping among the Beverly Hills boutiques in March 1978, the *Los Angeles Times* went, too – and headed its report simply 'Spring Spree'.

They pictured her handling a 'dreamy shoe' at Giorgio's while Stan discussed the purchase of a mansion on Sunset Boulevard. The Hermans also looked carefully over an antique diamond necklace. It was an important purchase and Linda treated it as such. 'Stan,' she said to her husband, feeling the jewels the way other women feel a fur collar on a coat, 'Stan I *need* this.' No one seemed to doubt the use of the word 'need' – least of all Frances Klein, who owned the shop.

Linda, practically single handed, it appeared, kept designer Dmitri in business at the Mr Guy boutique. She bought a number of his outfits and said she would wear them in her next film, *Avalanche Express*, which was to be shot in Germany. (In this, she would play an American agent involved in transporting a KGB chief to safety in the West.)

People could be forgiven if they thought that the outfits were more important than the film itself. She was certainly giving the impression of enjoying shopping a great deal more than she liked filming.

But she wasn't buying clothes for her husband. He wouldn't approve of that at all. 'Oh ne-ver. He'll never let me select clothes for him.' He, too, shopped at Dmitri. So did David Janssen, who had bought fifteen suits there.

Stan was coming to Germany to spend a month with his working wife.

But John's influence still permeated practically everything she did – every day that she did it. And that was why she was determined to maintain her friendship with his new and old wives.

As she was to say: 'I spent ten years of my life with John, Ursula spent nine. That's a long time. We loved him very much and if we didn't still have him around, those would be years forgotten. So it behoves us to keep him in our lives. We still love him, but we're no longer in love with him. Bo is in love with him. So there are no problems. Both Ursula and I have gone on to other loves and other lifestyles and we're not interested in going back to John; Bo knows that.'

The fact that Stan knew it – and accepted it – was the best part of it all.

Stan and John didn't exactly become firm friends themselves, but Herman seemed not to mind the great affection Linda obviously had for her former husband. The way she said it, there really wasn't much exception one could take. It seemed such a nice, kind sort of thing to say.

'Ursula and I can joke with Bo about her problems. We tell her that we understand. "We were there," we say.'

When Linda found that Bo had had a fight with John, both Linda and Ursula telephoned her to offer sympathy. They also called John and, in a combined operations campaign, told him to be kinder to his new wife. 'You're being far too strict,' they said – metaphorically nursing wounds they felt they had experienced themselves and on the same battle field.

Everything, Linda reported, had turned out fine.

There were few obvious problems in her own new marriage. Stan was plying her with gifts that John may have thought were unnecessary. Herman didn't make her waistcoats or boots, instead bought her Cadillacs and mink coats.

When Linda said she wanted to study cookery, he arranged for her to have a professional cook's kitchen and to learn from some of the finest culinary artists in the land.

Also she was working on that career and the jobs were starting to come in. Columnists came to interview her – including one man who was kinder than most about her abilities at the time: 'The average person's view of a Hollywood star is someone consumed with ambition, someone who struggles up the ladder, always scratching for success. And then there's Evans.'

But she still wasn't really a star. Back in 1974, she worked on *The Klansman* – which had been the original title of D. W. Griffith's *Birth of A Nation*.

This bore absolutely no relationship whatsoever to the Griffith classic. It was set in Alabama and the Ku Klux Klan figured widely in the story. That aside, there was no link whatsoever.

Linda was lost in a cast that began with Lee Marvin and Richard Burton and went on to include O. J. Simpson, Cameron Mitchell, Lola Falana, David Huddleston and Luciana Paluzzi.

The story about a sheriff's apparent private war with the sheet-covered Klansmen was dismissed by *Variety* in a sentence which even for toughly-worded Hollywood critics was devastating: 'There's not a shred of quality, dignity, relevance or impact in this yahoo-oriented bunk.'

Leslie Halliwell, who knows a thing or two about movies (his *Film Guide* and *Filmgoers' Companions* are justly regarded by movie buffs as of almost biblical significance) said it was a 'violent melodrama, all noise, brutality and bad acting.'

He didn't exempt Linda from this indictment and compounded the matter by putting the Evans name at the end of the exhaustive list of players in the piece.

All this didn't exactly reinforce her confidence in her own ability to be a star. But still that wasn't really what she was looking for.

She didn't need the trappings of stardom because she had them already. Linda would have liked to have been accepted as an actress, but she gave the impression of not minding a great deal if she continued to play in a few more bad movies like *The Klansman*, simply because it meant independence and a chance to work. As Mrs Stan Herman there was a definite risk of being just the decorative side of a highly successful businessman.

However, Linda liked being seen with Stan as much as he liked to have her around. They dined out regularly at such Beverley Hills nighteries as La Scala, the Bistro and Trader Vic's.

They also enjoyed in particular Pips. It wasn't surprising. Pips, a backgammon club – about the nearest to heavy gaming allowed in California – was jointly owned by Stan and *Playboy*'s owner Hugh Hefner. For lunch, they'd go to the Right Bank Upstairs. 'It's kinda fun up there for lunch,' she said, almost apologising for the money all this cost. 'It feels like we're on a trip or something. It's private and lovely.'

Certainly, there were a lot of people envious of Stan for being able to have all those 'private and lovely' occasions with Linda Evans, either in Beverly Hills during the week or at Malibu at week-ends.

A lot of her spare time was spent in shaping up – and her shape was still pretty exciting – on the tennis court or on the saddle of her bicycle. People didn't ride bicycles in Beverly

Hills because they had to. Linda did it purely for the fun – to feel the wind rustling around her legs and through her hair which somehow seemed to stay in place, if only in a careless way; the kind of way film directors liked to see on their pretty actresses. If only there had been more directors who wanted to see Linda's hair that way....

But like John Derek, Stan Herman wasn't keen on seeing his wife going out to work, even as a glamorous actress with at least a faint hope of stardom. And that was a problem.

It would have helped the still lingering self doubts that Linda felt about herself had he been more encouraging. As she has said: 'I was a late bloomer, I had been married nearly all my adult life, but I still didn't know who I was, what I believed or really wanted.'

The cars, the house and the dresses didn't provide any instant answers. Neither did the fact that they could travel anywhere in the world, first class, with a limousine to take them to and from all the airports they used.

Suddenly, with all the big things going so well, she missed the little ones. And being mistress to a house full of servants wasn't her idea of paradise, either.

As she was to recall: 'Just to sit there and have people wait on you is a very painful thing if you're not used to it.'

Sure, people would tell her how lucky she was, how much they envied her. 'But,' she said, 'when you're used to taking care of yourself and feel like you want to do your own part, it's a very bizarre thing to just let people iron and clean and do for you. Also to tell them things. I like people an awful lot and the first time I had to say to the housekeeper, "That's not been done properly and I want this and that and cook this and don't do that", I couldn't do it.'

She had an insatiable desire, she said, to go and do her own washing up. That was not a statement calculated to get potential audiences to identify with her.

But even with such problems, she was grateful to her husband. She would say: 'He helped me to learn to think for myself and I believe it was perfect for me to marry Stan when

I did. I wouldn't have missed a second of my life with him.'

But there were those problems of her domestic life. When she said 'I stepped back into the shadows to be a good wife,' she did so wistfully – even though she protested that nothing would make her regret that decision.

Even if she wasn't allowed to wash her own dishes.

When she and Herman hired a married couple as servants, she found it impossible to keep up with the help. They dressed for the part, he in tails and black tie, she in starched white apron and cap.

Linda found she had to put on a formal evening or cocktail dress and her jewellery, just so as not to disappoint her servants. She wanted to keep her jeans and silk blouse for the evening, too.

In the end, Herman said she should fire the couple – but she couldn't bring herself to do it.

Neither could she really understand his business – which she wasn't expected to do, but it caused additional frustration for a wife who, though in the shadows, liked to think she was intellectually able to grasp such matters.

Stan was quite happily cashing in on the successes of the town in which he lived.

As he said in 1977: 'There are people you've never heard of earning $50,000 a week with television series. And a whole lot of producers and directors are making $10,000 a week. Every star who has a come-back – and I know dozens personally – has meant work for a psychiatrist, an agent, an accountant – and a realtor.'

He wasn't including Linda in that bracket. He had no come-back in mind for her, although she would make a couple of attempts.

She was signed for an episode in NBC's *The Rockford Files*, with James Garner. Then with Chuck Connors, Robert Forster and Will Sampson she was featured in a TV movie set during the early 1930s called *Legend At Sundown*.

On the odd occasions when newspapermen showed any remote interest in her, it was still because she was Stan's wife.

An item in the *Los Angeles Times* in March 1978 reported that 'Stan and Linda Herman ... like to go to the Easter sunrise service at the Self-Realisation Fellowship in Pacific Palisades.' Which was interesting for a nice Jewish boy like Stan.

In an article on the prosperous real-estate business in *The State* newspaper, the writer Colin Dangaard described a visit to 'Stan Herman With Wife, Linda'. And that was already 1977.

The writer was fascinated by all the gossip Stan managed to pick up – 'enough ... to keep Rona Barrett busy for a month.' Yes, that was true. When houses were put on sale, it was often because a marriage was about to break up. 'I feel like a doctor or a lawyer,' said Stan, while Linda smiled contentedly and dutifully in the background. 'My position is privileged. I also know where the dollar is.' He knew so well where that dollar was that Linda only had to mention that there was something she liked, for it to be delivered to her within the hour.

That wasn't, however, what she was looking for at all.

So she went into analysis – with a woman named Patricia Sun. She wasn't laying on any psychiatrist's couch, instead, she was sitting in on a class in what was called 'psychological healing'.

Linda would claim that it worked. 'All my life, I'd been fighting my strength,' she said – as though she still saw being strong, mentally if not physically, as a totally unfeminine characteristic, with her mother's timidity still seen as the conventional, if regrettable, women's role model.

Suddenly it changed. 'To me, Pat was the perfect example of strength and gentleness. She helped me to see female strength in new light and gave me the courage to express it.'

If Stan had given her the same strength, their marriage might have worked out better.

They planned to have children. There were no youngsters from a previous marriage hanging around (to give them an excuse not to do so), but it didn't happen.

So Linda found different ways of occupying herself. Linda started numerology – which had been invented long before there was an America, let alone an American film or television industry.

It intrigued her that the ancient world had believed that a person's future could be predicted simply by linking up various numbers in their lives – like birth dates.

'It's a beautiful science,' she said, but wouldn't say more unless she had a whole evening in which to discuss it. Her favourite hobby-horse took some riding. More important, she thought she had found the secret of learning about herself. There were those who sometimes doubted that.

She still couldn't find a job, and inwardly the thing she did know about herself was that until she found one and could be her own woman, things weren't going to work out. One of Linda's closest friends told me that she was sleep-walking through her marriage to Herman. That may be a truthful assessment of it.

Since those days, it has become fashionable among her set of acquaintances to say that she was deliberately putting her career 'on hold' during this time. The truth is that she wasn't getting professional offers that meant anything to her. It is also clear that Stan Herman wouldn't be satisfied with having a wife who was anything but a top star, and there was very little prospect of that.

There was the same problem she had faced with John Derek. As she said: 'When I was with John, a part of me was totally closed off.' Now she was in a different cocoon, but a cocoon just the same.

Derek had constantly pushed Linda to 'improve'. Stan was pushing her to stay, as the song almost had it, as sweet as she was.

And she wasn't really helping herself. 'I resisted change most of my life because it frightened me. So I spent most of my life just trying to make everything very safe.'

Now that everything *was* safe for her, she wanted more.

'Letting go of this kind of fear involves going into yourself and finding that inner strength that has been locked away and that emerges only with the right stimulation.'

She knew she would only be happy if she *did* have the right stimulation. She had a marriage, which was far from ideal although she seemed to love Stan and he definitely adored her, but she didn't have children and she didn't really have a career.

Parts in *Nowhere to Run* with David Janssen and *Standing Tall* with Robert Forster didn't amount to very much.

So Linda took more lessons – this time on how to act. And she walked a well-trodden path, one that even Marilyn Monroe had travelled. She called on Lee Strasberg, who ran the world-famous Actors Studio.

The Studio pioneered The Method. It didn't convert Linda into a Method actress but she maintained it did help her to learn about herself. 'I had to find out what I didn't know. I had a lot of fear as a young person, thinking there were all sorts of things I didn't know.'

Now what she knew was that she was going to have to change the lifestyle which had given her plenty of riches but precisely no satisfaction at all. She and Stan Herman separated.

'Stan,' she finally decided, 'is not cut out for marriage.'

5

Linda would say that she was 'baffled' by the failure of her marriage to Stan Herman. 'The important thing is we're still friends,' she said soon after the collapse of the poor little rich couple's seemingly ideal state.

It seemed to fit in with the previous relationships and with what Stan said about his former wife himself. 'She holds on to the past,' he said. 'She saves every clipping and every old piece of clothing that John made for her. They didn't have any sentimental value ... She'd buy new things all the time but hold on to the old. She's very protective of her possessions, like a good chipmunk.' She held on to her memories of life with Herman, too.

Her explanation was simpler – and perhaps more romantic. 'I'm friendly with all my old beaux because, after all, we *have* shared a degree of love and intimacy.'

There were those who thought she had taken this love of the past a little too much to heart. When Ursula Andress had her first baby at forty-plus, mother, baby and new husband Harry Hamlin went to Linda's house to live for a time. The Hamlins' own house was too small. Linda simply thought it was the right thing to do. Ever since she had married Herman she decided to make the fullest use possible of the riches he had given her – and that included trying to share them, too. It did seem to be taking things too far, but she didn't think so, although she did look nostalgically to the past.

'My husband didn't have millions, but he had an awful lot,'

59

she would muse, remembering what suddenly was no longer hers. But none of that mattered very much. 'When you're raised in a middle-class family and suddenly experience the kind of money where you can have all the things you've ever wanted, you discover that wanting them is more exciting than getting them.'

No longer having Stan's money was not going to be her problem. What was impossible to fathom was why it all broke up.

When she did reflect on the reason, she came to the conclusion that the result had been inevitable. 'We did our best, but Stan had always led a single life, and that's the life he's most comfortable with.'

That bit about still being friends was very important to Linda; seemingly, it was the most important thing of all. She was still the best of friends, too, with John Derek, even with Bo, who was beginning to look more and more the way Linda had looked. Mr Derek was plainly a bespoke tailor as far as women were concerned, fashioning them the way he liked them to be.

In the film *10* Bo bared her very adequate breasts and wore her hair just as Linda had done at the time of the *Playboy* picture spread. And, it has to be confessed, was being noticed much more than Linda ever had.

As before, Linda protested that she had no resentment for the usurper any more than she would have done had there been a new Mrs Herman on the horizon. And neither did Ursula Andress: 'Some people who don't know us seem to think our friendship weird. They think we must all be under John's influence. Not at all. The truth is, he's a kind, loving man and we're determined to continue our relationship with him as a friend. If we didn't, we'd simply be denying ourselves a lot. It's as simple as that.'

There were those who saw an almost super-human righteousness in Linda's apparent acceptance of the situation and in her friendship with the new Mrs Derek. It seemed no different from the kind of friendship she protested she enjoyed with Ursula Andress.

Unusual? It was practically uncanny, particularly in the cynical world of Hollywood.

She regarded it as quite as simple to stay friendly with Stan, too, and to be grateful for all he had done for her. So grateful, in fact, that she didn't even press home a divorce suit. In the end, it was Stan who sued – but not until 1981.

Then Stan married again, and his wife Denise became the kind of friend Bo and Ursula had become. The new Hermans dined at the home of the former Mrs Herman as if they had always been good friends – and never anything more.

It seemed that one way of getting a friend for life was simply to marry Linda Evans. She wasn't going to let anyone go – simply because they had had the misfortune – or maybe fortune – of ending up in a divorce court together.

'I don't understand,' she maintains, 'why people when they find out they can't get along, can't still be friends. The qualities for which you married that person are still there.' And then she repeated: 'I always thought I'd marry once and for ever – but I wouldn't change even twenty seconds of my life. If I had to do it all over again, I'd do it exactly the same. I've learned from the good and the bad. The bad taught me well and made me strong.'

And what was more, she had found out how to be strong without losing her femininity. With Stan's help, she had beaten the old bug and had erased her mother's example from her mind.

Perhaps secretly she was most afraid of the usurper Bo doing so much better than she had ever done in show business. Then it would become embarrassing. With that thought in mind, she started more seriously to look for work – now without Stan hovering in the background and vetoing (always for her own good, of course) anything that came her way.

Avalanche Express had been at just the right time for her – beginning in the dying days of her marriage and finishing as far as filming was concerned, when it was all over.

The story got itself derailed before the film ended and, indeed almost landed in a siding during production. Robert Shaw, its director and chief star, died while the movie was still being shot and even his dialogue had to be dubbed by another actor (Robert Rietty) before it could be released.

Lee Marvin, Maximillian Schell, Mike Connors, Horst Buchholtz and the former American footballer, Joe Nameth, all appeared, too – but this time Linda Evans was the undoubted female star, with third billing after Messrs Shaw and Marvin. In fact, she was the *only* female star.

It did her a lot of good – for her own ego – although she was to say shortly before the movie went into the cinemas: 'When I work, I give it everything I have. But when I'm not working, I'm not restless to push on to bigger and better parts.'

For that reason, she was trying to extend her abilities. She knew there were weaknesses in her professional repertoire – most of all in her voice; her singing voice that is.

She took lessons from a coach, who for five months got her doing practically nothing but 'ooh' and 'aah'. She, for her part, did nothing more at this time than cry – and cry and cry.

Linda knew that her sister had been right in summing up her inability to hold a note, and when she thought about it, she cried some more. But finally she sang a whole song. When she did, she told herself: 'I have a lovely voice'. There were those who saw a kind of Trilbyesque characteristic in what happened, but happen it did. When she finished the song, she cried again – 'but,' as she explained, 'this time out of joy.'

There was no overwhelming ambition burning inside her, she protested over and over again. But when an offer came from Warner Bros. to make *Tom Horn*, she accepted with the kind of alacrity which might not have been considered altogether ladylike.

It wasn't, it might have been thought, a totally tempting role to a girl who seemed to be at her best when she could look beautiful. In this, she had to appear with a tooth missing and a gold replacement in her gums. Not really very nice at all.

(The gold tooth wasn't all that obvious. The cameraman said he hated it and took it as a personal challenge to find ways of covering it up.)

Her wardrobe was horrendously expensive – each of the dresses would, ironically, cost a great deal more than those in a certain T V series that would follow, but they were the dreariest any star had ever been asked to wear since Olivia de Havilland battled with *The Snake Pit*.

'Every one of them was custom made,' Linda explained – as if that really explained anything. But such is the way of Hollywood studios and the money they spend.

She liked the film and the lack of requirement to spend hours in make-up. 'I'd get up in the morning, brush my teeth, take a shower, stick my hair in a bun and go to work. It was such a pleasure.'

Warner Bros. who released the film, and First Artists, who produced it, seemed to take the whole thing in their corporate stride.

Now, she wasn't just the third star, but co-star with Steve McQueen in one of his last roles, one in which it was said he, too, had lost all his old glamour.

It was a pity because they both suffered the fate of the rest of the movie and went down with the ship.

It was McQueen himself who insisted that Linda wore no make-up for the part and did the kind of things to her hair which ladies only experienced when being pulled by a tractor through the foliage, or perhaps the maze at Hampton Court.

In *Tom Horn*, described as the story of one of the 'last great heroes of the American West', Linda played Glendoline Kimmel, a woman who came to Wyoming, in search of romance and found instead, Mr Horn. He was a former member of the gallant United States Cavalry who became an equally gallant detective; gallant that was, in the eyes of the audience, but not in those of the law. He ended up framed for murder and standing on the scaffold.

He was also framed by Linda – who nevertheless liked McQueen very much. She found him reclusive to the point of paranoia. But he was nice to her and she confessed she enjoyed making love to him on screen. A lot more than the critics liked watching the film.

Variety said of this picture: 'Imagine a film that opens up with dialogue that can't be heard at all, then proceeds to build up to a fist fight that's never seen, that cuts away to sunsets to fill in other scenes that have no dramatic point, that presents a meal where the sound of knives and forks drowns out what's being said, and you have just the beginning of what's wrong with *Tom Horn*.'

But it was important for her to have done that film, to have been called a star – even with such lack of critical acclaim.

Very few people knew of her self doubts. As she said: 'Everyone always thought I had myself together. But I didn't. I've been married since I was twenty-one. My life has always been us, not me. I really didn't know what I wanted.'

She was now thirty-seven and if people wanted to know what a woman of that age was doing seeking the glamorous life of a movie star, this was their justification. Yes, Linda could try to act – Strasberg training notwithstanding, she wasn't really succeeding as a great actress – but she should not pretend that at her age she could excite people with her beauty. People just weren't interested in women of thirty-seven – were they?

It certainly didn't help in any need she felt to get back on equal terms with Bo Derek. But then, perhaps, Linda didn't want to get on equal terms with her.

The 5'8" tall – six inches taller than Bo – Linda Evans was telling people now that she was taking her career into her own hands. There's no doubt that neither John nor Stan would have welcomed her playing the schoolmistress involved with McQueen in *Tom Horn*.

Linda herself seemed happy with the role of the shiny-faced teacher, even though it wasn't attracting the slightest kind of attention from the critics.

'I've always been protected by men,' she said. 'Now I feel I'm in charge of my life.' She said it in an interview in *People* magazine, a publication that was as amazed at the turn of events as anyone else.

The real significance of the interview was simply that a

As Alexis Carrington, Joan Collins was not only a rival for Krystle's husband but also for Linda's stardom in the series.

Now both Joan and Linda have established a close friendship and are generous in their admiration for each other.

Linda much enjoyed her part as a western saloon singer in the TV film *The Gambler* (1984).

Linda has always enjoyed a healthy lifestyle and has had a gym built into her Beverly Hills home.

Linda is the author of two books on beauty and exercise, and is a shining example of practising what you preach.

Linda's favourite fur sweater – a snip at $3,400.

Filmed in a French château, no expense was spared in a commercial for the perfume 'Forever Krystle'.

With Stefanie Powers (*left*) in a recent TV film *Butch Cassidy Rides Again.*

magazine of its calibre thought it important enough to feature her.

Life was quite obviously getting better for Linda. She had bought a $750,000 French provincial 'cottage' in Coldwater Canyon, a long winding road leading upward from the most fashionable part of Beverly Hills, close to the Beverly Hills Hotel. It's a road with its quota of stars, old and new, including then the California retreat of gangster star James Cagney.

Buying a new property meant keeping in touch with her ex-husband. She enjoyed their meetings. 'Stan still makes my heart jump when he enters a room,' she said.

But she wouldn't have wanted to go back to him, even if he and Denise had not now married. Linda was making it clear she liked being what a generation or two earlier would have been described as a 'bachelor girl'. 'I find it dangerous but exhilarating,' she said.

There was more television work for her, including the *Hunter* series. In this, she starred opposite James Franciscus. Both played Federal agents. The series was no great hit, but it was positioned by CBS in place of the *Executive Suite* shows which had not done well enough in the ratings battles.

'Spies,' said Linda. 'I love it. Being a Scorpio, you know, it's me.'

It was during this stage in her career that it suddenly dawned on people that the Linda Evans they were watching now could – just could – be the same girl who wore that two-piece bathing suit playing opposite Frankie Avalon on the sands of *Beach Party*. Could she also be the one who played the daughter of Barbara Stanwyck?

One writer wrote to the *Los Angeles Times*: 'I have watched for years, but haven't seen Linda Evans of *The Big Valley* in any show. Now a Linda Evans shows up on the *Hunter* series. She doesn't look like the said girl. What happened to the girl I saw on *The Big Valley*?'

It seemed a not altogether unfair question – and was very much a vindication of all John Derek had done for her. But the paper answered: 'It's the same actress. She just grew up.'

And Linda had done that all right, although there was still a touch of innocence about her, a feeling of unworldliness about her demeanour and the things she sometimes said – particularly about religion. Few would argue when she said that God was responsible for everything she did. She would say things like: 'I had a talk with Him while I was driving over here.'

She would hope that her listeners would accept what she said. The one thing she wouldn't have wanted was for people to laugh at her – or, worse, pity her. Saying those things about God was an intellectual decision.

'When I was a little girl,' she would say, 'people used to say, "Linda, you're so pretty." They never said, "Linda, you're so smart." That was what they told my elder sister and sure enough, she went on to be class valedictorian.'

So really that was what it was: she had always been labouring under an inferiority complex and was determined that somehow, some day, people would think that she wasn't quite as shallow as the impression she gave.

With the marriage to Stan – and he always made her feel he was very clever while she was perhaps a little dumb – now behind her, she was doing all she could to convince herself to change things.

Four years after leaving Herman she thought she had done it. 'Now, I've found the joy of learning about myself and others and I'm still growing, learning to stand up for myself. I know love is more important than success or money or fame. But if I don't find it, it will not destroy me.'

Nothing, it seemed, *could* destroy her or her outlook on life. Yet she wasn't really content. 'I'm happiest when I'm in love and sharing my life with someone. I would be a wonderful housewife.'

But that wasn't her lot, and she wasn't sure whether she liked it or not. 'It's an interesting place' – Linda was apparently confusing geography with her marital state – 'because it's new to me.' And, she reminded those who wanted to hear, 'I've been married practically all my life.'

Now, quite suddenly, there was something else happening to her life. There was an offer on its way which seemed to say that stardom – at last – was more likely than Linda becoming a housewife.

6

Feminists wouldn't like to hear it, but it must be said that men have been the principal influence on the career of Linda Evans. First her father, then her two husbands, and in 1981, the figure once more of Jay Bernstein.

Bernstein, the man who fifteen years earlier had tried unsuccessfully to create a public image for Linda, now decided to use her in a new kind of representative role, not at all the kind to which she had become accustomed.

Bernstein had had some experience in that field, long after licking the wounds of the failed Linda Evans campaign. He had gone on to manage Farah Fawcett, who had been described as 'The Perfect thirty-year-old'. (As Bernstein told me: 'Before that, nobody had dared think of a thirty-year-old as being perfect at all. There were always those perfect at twenty-five like Elizabeth Taylor in *A Place In The Sun* and before that Jane Russell in *The Outlaw*.)

All of a sudden, thanks to the shrewd pushing of the publicity-minded Mr Bernstein, it became fashionable to admit you were thirty.

The slightly older woman breathed a sigh of relief.

It was then that Dr Joyce Brothers, stepped in. She was a woman who then, as now, made a living out of telling other women – and not a few men – who read her books, saw her television programmes or listened to her advice line on the radio, that there were ways of solving whatever problems they cared to create.

Bernstein met the attractive but middle-aged Dr Brothers who came to him with a simple request: 'It would be really wonderful if you could adapt what you do for thirty-year-olds to women of forty.'

'I thought it was a great idea,' said Bernstein. 'After all, the average age of women in America was then forty.'

It was a time when women were engaged in matters like abortion and equal rights. At least, that is what the media said women were interested in. Bernstein took up Dr Brothers's theory and came to the conclusion that there were other young middle-aged women who were more interested in staying feminine and looking beautiful.

It was in the midst of all this theorising, that he met Linda at a cocktail party. 'Seeing her was the revelation. I realised that she was the perfect example of how I could promote a woman of forty and make other people want to be like her.'

He confirmed what he really already knew. Linda was doing a fair amount of work that provided her with plenty of exposure but no impact. If she wanted to advance her career, she had to have more going for her.

'We got talking,' Bernstein recalled for me. 'I told her that there were ways of both doing more for herself and helping women of her age. That got her interested.'

He could see the thoughts surging through Linda's head. Finally, a smile crept round her lips. 'Well ...' she said. 'If it would really help women. ...'

Bernstein replied: 'It would not only help women, but would do you a great deal of good, too.'

He wanted to take Linda under his wing – not in the way of a John Derek or a Stan Herman. He had no sexual intent. It was going to be a business arrangement from which both would benefit equally.

They came to an agreement. 'It wasn't a whole lot of fun,' he said. 'It was very hard work. Until then, nothing she did really stood out. She always looked good, but no one was really paying much attention to her.'

Jay began his campaign on television. There was a top TV

show called *Twenty-Twenty*. The programme had scheduled a feature on Bernstein's business acumen. It was a good opportunity to get off the ground his new role as personal manager to Linda Evans.

'I turned it all on Linda,' he told me. It worked. She was suddenly in demand on other shows, too. One was called *The Battle of the Network Stars*, in which show biz personalities became athletes for the programme's duration. Linda looked great in her white shorts.

She still wasn't sure she wanted to do much else, helping American womanhood notwithstanding. But Bernstein persisted.

He told her: 'Bo Derek is 10. You can be 20!' She accepted the offer and did more shows.

Then, later in 1981, ABC announced they were going to do a play called *Oil*. If people liked it, the network was prepared to turn it into a series.

No one doubted that the aim was indeed to turn it into a series – to cash in on the phenomenal success of the rival network CBS's *Dallas*. *Dallas* had an apparently magic ingredient, a rambustious and thoroughly nasty individual called JR, played by Larry Hagman, who until that role had been best known for his part in a much earlier series called *I Dream of Jeannie*, but perhaps best of all for simply being veteran star Mary Martin's son.

There were two beautiful women, Victoria Principal and the older Linda Gray. Victoria had made a tremendous impact, but Linda Gray really hadn't, apart from looking pretty and crying a lot on screen.

But the real significance of the show was its emphasis on phenomenal wealth. No one – or at least very few – could identify with such riches, but there were millions who liked looking at the clothes, the jewels and just watching people who took fabulous wealth for granted.

There was a certain emphasis on the source of that wealth – oil, but for most of the time it was incidental; the family (all, strangely and without ever any reasonable explanation being offered, living not just on the same estate, Southfork, but also in the same house), the wealth and the in-fighting became the more vital factors.

ABC now planned to cream off that market itself. If *Oil* worked, its own stars would be as important as Larry Hagman, Victoria Principal, Linda Gray or anyone else who ever appeared in that Texas-based 'soap'.

The basic ingredients were going to be the same – enormous wealth, family conflict, big houses, big cars and actors and actresses who would become big stars. Pretty obviously, it couldn't be set in Dallas. But it had to be in another real city, even if it were the kind of amorphous community which no one would altogether recognise. There would be lots of standard fill-in shots of shiny skyscrapers reflecting the sun.

It was decided that Denver, Colorado, would fit the bill perfectly. It was quite reasonable to have people based in Denver, wasn't it? Anything, it seemed, would be better than yet another series or even a single show based in San Francisco or Los Angeles.

The idea had come from Richard and Esther Shapiro, who had been working together since their marriage twenty years earlier.

They had been approached by TV tycoon Aaron Spelling, the nearest thing to a Hollywood mogul that the television industry had yet thrown up, with productions of dubious artistic value, but undoubtedly commercial viability like *The Love Boat* and *Charlie's Angels* behind him.

Esther was the one to accept the challenge first. 'I like to create characters who are always trying to gain control of their lives,' she has explained. She also liked 'writing about Middle America'. She meant in the geographical sense, of course.

Bernstein heard about *Oil*, as anyone else in the business would have done, and immediately realised that the leading woman's part of the fiancée to the oil tycoon could fit Linda like the shoes she bought from Giorgio.

Spelling was impressed with Bernstein's suggestion and sent Linda a copy of the script for what was now going to be a two-hour production.

'It's not a series,' said Linda. 'Is it?'

She had to be told that no, it wasn't. But it might be – and everyone at ABC and in the Aaron Spelling organisation hoped it would be. Linda was hesitant. She didn't want to do another *Hunter* series in which she would be lost among the action, the scenery or the male stars.

Spelling told her that it would be unlikely. She would play an important part, look extraordinarily elegant and ladylike and, besides, the money would be very, very good.

That bit about being elegant impressed her. She was fresh from *Tom Horn* and rejoiced that nobody would now expect her to have a gold tooth. Not only that, she would wear attractive dresses and her hair would be just the way she wanted to have it – even if she didn't yet know how that would be.

Spelling was the keenest of all to have Linda involved in his new 'baby'. He had been sending her scripts for months, although she had never actually gone to see him to talk about any of them.

'Don't forget,' said Bernstein who was hovering on the sidelines all the time, 'what you are doing for other women close to forty.'

It may not have been the gallant thing to do to keep reminding a woman of her age – or at least the age she was fast approaching – but Jay had to convince Linda that her responsibility to other women could make her more than one kind of symbol.

Before long it worked. Linda needed no persuading. 'I fell in love with the character,' she said. 'She was so like me.'

The time would come – and not many years afterwards – when she would say the exact opposite, but for the moment the reason she liked Krystle was because of that supposed affinity.

And certainly there would be similarities to the role she had played as Mrs Stan Herman. Then, she had been mistress of a big house who was expected to wear fine clothes – if only by the servants – and adapt to a lifestyle that hadn't always been hers.

To be fair, Linda said she thought Krystle was like her for different reasons.

'She was so much like me in a situation where she would have to stand on her own, speak for herself and develop as a person.'

The statement fitted in with her character quite as much as anything Krystle was to do.

Oil was a production fraught with problems. That is usually the case. In this case, it was more so than usual. Ninety per cent of the production had been filmed when trouble bubbled up like newly-discovered oil.

As regular addicts of the show soon found out, the story was of a fabulously rich oil baron, his family and his intrigues. At about the time Linda accepted the part of what was then the baron's fiancée – her name was Krystle Jennings – the male lead was sorted out, too.

This was the role of Blake Carrington, the ruthless, elegant man about Denver who presumably could buy out the rest of the town with a flick of the switch on the mahogany intercom system on his imported French desk. It went to George Peppard, then fifty-two years old (he always looked much younger) and veteran of many important Hollywood films ranging from *Breakfast at Tiffany's* to *The Blue Max*.

Peppard never seemed happy with the role and finally with just that ten per cent of filming to go, he left the production. He simply couldn't take any more. The idea of expanding the role to a week-by-week series was no more his scene than Linda thought it was going to be hers.

A replacement had to be found. He was John Forsythe, whom Jay Bernstein had got to know well from his role in *Charlie's Angels*. In that series, Forsythe had been heard and not seen – and for long his identity was a closely-kept secret. He was Charlie, the man who gave instructions by tape and telephone to his Angels.

Blake Carrington was a different kind of part, and not just because he *was* now to be seen. Carrington was a hard, ruthless man. Before, Forsythe had always seemed to be Mr Nice Guy. That was why he had even had his own TV series called *The*

John Forsythe Show. They didn't give programmes like that to people whom audiences have to learn to hate. *The Ambassador's Daughter* and *The Trouble With Harry*, in which he appeared with a very young Shirley MacLaine in her first ever film role, confirmed this.

Blake Carrington wasn't going to be a real Nasty, but there were things about him that were not thought to be endearing to ladies with sensitive natures.

Linda had quite plainly never been quite so happy – professionally speaking – before. And she said it was all because she did so closely identify with Krystle. 'The woman I play', she said, now that the theories of the script had been replaced by the reality of the actual filming, 'just follows her emotions, not using her head at all.'

But she was beginning to change her opinion that she and Krystle were so alike. 'I love the part because I was there once. I hope the character will grow just as I have.'

She could have no idea just how much the character and the factors connected with it would grow.

Everything about *Oil* was lavish. Part of Linda's wardrobe as Krystle was a ten-carat diamond ring. She was delighted. It was the kind of sparkler Stan might have bought her, the kind she really appreciated. Everyone seemed to appreciate it – apart, that is, from Aaron Spelling's wife, Candy. 'That's only a *small* diamond,' Mrs Spelling protested. Aaron took the hint and ordered an 18-carat rock to replace it.

Oil worked. All *three* hours of it, as it became.

Linda had now become the role model for all forty-year-old women that Jay Bernstein had predicted.

ABC picked up its options and a new series was commissioned. The only trouble was that name. *Oil*, warned the people who advised on such things, may not give the right impression. To the makers it may have represented wealth and success. But to others, the word 'oil' could be associated with greasy black hair and unfortunate complexions.

A conference was held and a new name was dreamed up for the series and accepted – *Dynasty*.

7

It was billed as a 'compelling new series created to be an involving and continuing part of your life.'

The nation – or nations; because it became a breath-bating talking point on five continents – could come to a halt on the night *Dallas's* JR was shot, (such claims for TV supersoaps were not as outrageous as this immediately sounded). But could another series have the same impact?

Both Spelling and ABC thought there was a good chance that it could.

There was John Forsythe, with his blue rinse, offering distinguished authority as the oil tycoon Blake Carrington; the sort of success figure on whom the sun could be guaranteed never to set.

But everything seemed to be focussing around his attractive fiancée with that intriguing name Krystle. No, the public were subtly told, not Crystal, Krystle. There weren't many Krystles around and the way Linda Evans was going to play her, she was going to be positively unique.

John Derek was going to be proud of her. Even in 1981, six years after her divorce, the thought wasn't going to be totally absent from her mind.

But as Jay Bernstein predicted, she was going to be a different sort of leading lady. So, now, there *were* to be subtle changes for The Woman Derek Had Made. Her dresses would be longer than anything his little Bo now wore. The shoulders would be wider. And if she showed anything of her breasts – and the limitations on doing so on prime-time were considerable – it would be limited to what used to be known as cleavage.

The design department seemed fairly confident that her styles were going to be copied by other women and watched very carefully by men, too.

As for her part in the story, well ... did the story really matter?

In truth, she still worried about continuing, if only for the risks involved in tying herself down to something the makers anticipated would last for five years – in the event it would be still going strong after its fifth anniversary.

'I wasn't particularly interested in television work,' she would still affirm. However, she added, 'the prospect of dressing up and wearing pretty clothes as Krystle seemed a tempting chance to show people that I didn't look plain and fat all the time.'

And she added: 'When I decided to do *Dynasty*, there was no one else in my life ... it wasn't the first time I put my career first.'

The public wanted to see the things the Carringtons' money bought and enjoy the problems resulting from the intrigue that was promised.

After all, as the early publicity revealed, Blake Carrington ruled an empire. The rod he used to do so may have been made of gold-plated iron, but that didn't guarantee he could fight the problems his family, his 'dynasty', brought him.

As for Krystle, she hardly knew what she was letting herself in for. She didn't fit into the mansion, and that was for sure. She didn't know how to run the house, almost what cutlery to use, and the butler Joseph enjoyed every moment of her discomfort.

The emotions, the tugs of war – the not-so-nice way Blake's son Stephen, played by Al Corley, carried on, brought difficulties. His bitter relationship with Blake's daughter Fallon (it was as though the writers had gone through a dictionary of names and had either deliberately made up most of the important ones or had looked for the most obscure), played by Pamela

Sue Martin, led to ... well, bitterness.

Linda was told her character would go through numerous changes, which worried her a bit. What sort of changes? No one could really be sure. And that worried her even more. As she explained: 'I really dislike being unhappy, so the last thing I wanted to do was to cry and be depressed at work. I had to decide if I wanted to spend five years going in a direction I was unwilling to follow before. But Krystle was idealistic and I believed love would cure all things. That's what drew me to the part.'

Then there was Matthew Blaisdel (Bo Hopkins) in love with his boss's wife, and Walter Lankershim (Dale Robertson) an old-style oil man who didn't fit into Blake Carrington's suave velvet-gloved approach to big business.

But what sort of an impact would the serial make? Certainly, people reading the *Los Angeles Times*, the day the show opened on January 11, 1981, couldn't be sure.

The paper didn't even get the name right. The three-hour pilot *Oil* was now being marketed under the new title and would serve as an introduction to the series that was going to follow. What title was that? The *Times* seemed to think it was called *Destiny*. What Mr Spelling and the big noises of ABC thought when they read a detailed review headed 'Rendezvous With Destiny' must be left to the imagination. The next line read: '*Destiny* is a programme that dares to ask the question – "Can sex and opulence replace Monday Night Football?"'

It may have been a question worth asking. But *Destiny*? That was what the paper called it. The destiny of *Dynasty* was the top talking point in the industry – but to actually call it *Destiny*? The old adage that it didn't matter what people said about you, just so long as they spelt your name right might have been said to have applied to TV as to any branch of public life (on the other hand, it might not; crucifying a television programme in a review, even one that got the name right, could kill the baby before it learned to crawl.) This didn't bode at all well for what the makers hoped would be a household name as well as a household product.

The show, said Cecil Smith in his review, made the folks from *Dallas* 'look like sharecroppers'. Blake's home – which was now diagnosed as being a replica of the Filoli mansion close to San Mateo, Los Angeles – was described by the magazine as being perhaps the most sumptuous in TV history. If it really were based on Filoli it would have to be.

That mansion was built by a 1915 silver baron. The name came from the initials of the words that summed up everything he considered good – 'Fighting, Loving and Life.' That certainly would go a long way towards explaining what *Dynasty* would be about.

The house was all but moved to the Twentieth-Century Fox lot where the series was to be shot. The art director, John E. Chilberg, took a team of technicians to the mansion – designated as a 'national trust' – and together they made a series of impressions of carvings and panelling, with the same kind of material dentists use to take impressions for false teeth.

A total of $12,000 was spent in just collecting the brassware used in the sets. All the main rooms, the corridors and what became the famous staircase, all existed at San Mateo. Two smaller rooms were, however, added by the team – for they considered the dining room and living room in *Dynasty* had to be more comfortable than anything that existed in Filoli.

The bed they used was a genuine nineteenth-century four-poster. But it was turned into a king-size to accommodate both Linda and her screen husband.

But what impressed the *Los Angeles Times* reporter most was the *Dynasty* attitude to morality. It was, the reporter claimed, 'a hotbed of sex'.

Carrington was a 'randy old goat' and Fallon 'pops in and out of beds like a jumping jack. We meet her on horseback and when her horse tosses her in a stream she sheds her clothes and borrows her father's coat to cover her, a coat she quickly doffs when she meets the family chauffeur (Wayne Northrup) in the garage.'

As for Krystle, she was 'wonderfully endowed'. Indeed she was. But the kind of sex in which she was going to be involved –

although Mr Smith couldn't yet know such important and vital information – would be softer, subtler and, in many ways, sexier than one would have, at first, imagined.

Mr Smith was optimistic. 'Although produced in the languorous style for the soaps, this seems better than most – its script by Esther and Richard Shapiro seems less ridiculous than most of these lugubrious tales.... But when you watch this ménage and *Dallas* and *Flamingo Road* and *Secrets of Midland Heights*, one thought occurs – *Peyton Place*, by comparison, was high drama.'

But, inevitably, there was high drama, too, behind the scenes. Where did the show go from here?

Variety, who dubbed the soap opera a 'sudserama' seemed to think it could go a fair way. It described the production by Philip Parslow as 'handsome' and in 'another league' compared with *Dallas*. (So much in a different league that CBS were said to be very worried indeed about it.)

But there were other criticisms – 'contrived inter-relationships in which there's mightily little room for fun. ...'

'Forsythe's Blake so far remains the solid, slightly square businessman, while Linda Evans as Krystle ... seems destined to forgive and forget slights whenever Blake, trotting out posies and his private jet, flies her off to dinner ...'

There was as much public interest in the launch of the 'sudserama' as there had been about the first flight of a jumbo jet. Plans for a new space shuttle just didn't get anywhere by comparison.

Papers in the Los Angeles area were quick to quote all the shops who contributed to this new event that was so vitally important to every civilised human being this side of the Urals.

A more educated and informed note from the fashion staff of the *Los Angeles Times* revealed: 'Linda Evans plays Forsythe's wife – a woman who wears only big-name designer clothes. Pamela Sue Martin plays Forsythe's daughter by a former marriage, who hates her daddy's new wife but loves the beautiful furs, clothes and jewels she can buy with her daddy's money ... Furs on the series are from Edwards-Lowell in Beverly Hills.

Costumes are by Nolan Miller, with additional clothes by Calvin Klein, Anne Klein and scads of other hotsy-totsy New York fashion folk.'

Yes, the show was being noticed, and had a clear identity. There was the fashion, the great photography, the nice-looking women, the promise of intrigue. And when everyone wasn't intriguing? Well, with the fashion, the great photography, the nice-looking women and the promises ... it didn't seem to matter very much. Until, that is, very early on, it all seemed to get a little bogged down.

For a time, it seemed that *Dynasty* was running into the trap of being virtually interchangeable with *Dallas*, except that the characters didn't wear cowboy boots and Stetsons and really *were* so much better dressed (why, one asked however, did Blake wear that same dowdy blue cardigan in episode after episode? But you weren't expected to ask that, any more than *Dallas* freaks were intended to bother too much about the Ewing clan having only one house to live in). There *were* those same helicopter scenes, the same cuts in and out of the shiny skyscrapers. *Dallas* had its Cattle Barons Club, which was essentially a restaurant into which the big, nouveau-riche ranchers and a sprinkling of oil men poured like their gushing wells. *Dynasty* had a hotel, which was also essentially a restaurant. This was La Mirage. (Yes, the writers and the network *were* informed it should have been *Le* Mirage, but decided not to make any subtle changes.)

Does there, contemporary *Dynasty* addicts may ask, appear to be something or someone missing? It would take a year or more before that question was answered, so there is no point in answering it here. For the moment, audiences had to content themselves with a lovely, romantic, Hollywood-type wedding.

There were all the expected 'ahs' and 'oohs' when Krystle walked down the aisle and stood by Blake's side. It was the most spectacular and most publicised of Linda's weddings and in those early episodes it was shown to be just as fraught as any real-live romance she had had.

Krystle was, for instance, still in love with Blake's geologist employee (Bo Hopkins) who had come back from the Middle East after being sent off by revolutionaries ('militant radicals' they were dubbed). She had assumed *he* would be her husband – till he cleared the way for a marriage to Carrington by telling her he wouldn't leave his mentally-ill wife. Even so, she pawned her emerald necklace to get him out of trouble.

Naturally, Blake didn't like that at all. But, even less did he like her reluctance to have his baby.

Now that, too, provided a certain degree of conflict among the people guiding the destinies of both Linda-Krystle–Evans and of *Dynasty*, the soap you wouldn't want to put down.

Could she, on the one hand, be the attractive standard bearer – or even chest-barer – of the over-forties and on the other hand be expected to get involved with a pregnancy? All the medical advice pointed out that that could be fraught with problems. On the other hand, Linda herself was desperate to have a child of her own. Could she really allow herself to be broody in real life and yet reluctant to have a baby on 'the tube'? It was an insoluble problem. But it is of such problems that fortunes are made.

Dynasty looked as if it might do that, too. Yet it required a certain degree of faith. The show finished its first year thirty-eighth in the ratings. Nothing sensational, only just respectable, and dangerously close to ditching. The network decided, however, to keep it going.

People *were* talking about the show. And, most gratifying to Linda, they seemed to be talking mostly about her – and the clothes she wore.

In Denbigh, North Wales, just as in Denver, North Colorado, women were buying in chain stores dresses with high shoulders and low necks. Those hair dressers on five continents were being asked to produce back-combed styles like Krystle's.

What was different about Blake Carrington at this stage of the show's life was that he had become a very unpleasant character – no wonder Krystle wouldn't have his baby! – suave blue rinse notwithstanding.

As Linda said: 'It's so hard for me to take what he does

seriously because I know what a heart he has.'

There were also some other things that had to be taken seriously – like in September 1981 when Linda was bitten by a leopard while practising a circus act for a TV special – *The Circus of The Stars.* She was alone in a cage with two leopards, using a whip to coax them to do a few tricks, when she was bitten – as the papers joyfully reported – 'just below the breast.' Some would say that working in *Dynasty* could be even harder.

But it was Linda's heart that people wanted to see. Suddenly – quite suddenly, considering the previous reluctance of the media to take complete and satisfying notice of her – she was important.

People wanted interviews with Linda Evans. They needed to photograph her for magazines, to feature her on their covers. And, perhaps most significantly, they were wanting her for work.

Very cleverly – and Linda had good reason to be grateful for Jay Bernstein in this – she was now determined to not merely content herself with *Dynasty.*

She went to Fiji, to make an episode of *The Love Boat* series. The programme took her to Japan and Hong Kong, too. It also took her professional image a stage further. She played a gold digger in the show. 'I get to be mean and sneaky,' she told people enthusiastically, almost as enthusiastically as she spoke of how she and the rest of the cast were being paid to take an exotic cruise.

It added another dimension to her career.

By this time a great many people were taking *Dynasty* very seriously indeed. 'They're living weekly with these characters and vicariously experiencing their lives,' Linda said. It was 'almost like having friends next door.'

Henry Winkler, the leather-coated loveable rogue of television teen-age programmes, once told her that his wife used to shout at the set when she thought that Krystle was being ill-treated. When she believed that Blake was cheating on her, Mrs Winkler used to regale the set with invective. 'How dare he!' she'd say, glaring at the tube. 'Leave him! Divorce him!'

The role was beginning to change Linda, like it or not. Her lifestyle, aided by a phenomenal salary – details of which have never been released but is believed to be about $20,000 a week – was altering, and she was no longer apologising for it.

She began to wear the kind of clothes she wore on screen, even so early on in her *Dynasty* career.

She borrowed the clothes she wore on screen – as they all did on the cast of *Dynasty* – and went to parties in those longish dresses with the plunging necklines. Her shoulders were getting higher and more padded and those were the dresses she seemed to be favouring when she searched among the clothes rails in the studio wardrobe department.

However she didn't wear the deep, curve-caressing dresses and certainly not the jewellery from *Dynasty* when she went shopping. But neither did she now confine herself to those jeans and simple blouses when she mingled with the crowds in the Los Angeles markets. As she said: 'People expect Krystle to appear the way she does on television, so if I go shopping without make-up and with my hair in a pony tail, I hear people saying things like, "Is she or isn't she?"'

On the whole, though, she didn't go shopping at all. Most of her groceries and other food purchases were delivered. And there *were* advantages to being so well known and easily recognised. Head waiters knew her as readily as did lesser mortals. Seeing her approach the plush red cord was a signal for an instant placing at one of the best tables in the place. If a table wasn't available, somehow one would be brought. If she wanted to see a show, 'house' seats that didn't exist a minute before were suddenly conjured from nowhere.

She understood the human side of *Dynasty* and of Krystle herself. 'To see (Krystle) come into this dazzling new world – it's how we'd react if the Queen of England invited us to live at the palace. Fear of doing the wrong thing, not knowing when we're out of line. Krystle has no idea of what is going on.'

What Linda cherished most of all, it seemed, was her relationship with the other members of the cast – not least of all, her *Dynasty* husband, John Forsythe. The first Christmas of the show she sent him a present thanking him for 'by far the happiest marriage I have ever had.'

Forsythe seems to have taken his responsibility perhaps a little too seriously. He was quoted at this time saying that Linda had married 'inferior men'. She didn't like that at all, and said so.

'He doesn't even know my husbands. I think he ought to meet them before he says they're inferior.'

But she soon forgave him. He was nice to her and she thought he was very handsome – 'far more attractive than when I worked with him years ago.'

Dynasty was now seen in more than fifty countries. But even that wasn't really enough. Thirty-eighth in the domestic ratings was a situation that had to be improved on. There were long-into-the-night conferences between the ABC directors, Aaron Spelling and the Shapiros.

They had already made Blake's son Stephen a homosexual, which was considered extremely daring at the time and, sure, people were talking about it. But that still wasn't enough to bring *Dynasty* to the number-one spot, which was what everyone concerned was aiming at in the second year.

One reason, it was suggested, was that the story really wasn't exciting enough. True, there were good and bad characters, and they did have their share of shouting matches; but they were fighting without conviction. There was no one everyone wanted to hate, the way they hated JR. There weren't any people around who could be guaranteed to bring out a gun at the drop of a balance sheet.

Those who did fight were doing so against a bland brick wall, a nicely decorated brick wall, perhaps, but nothing that could be guaranteed to raise hackles, make the hair stand up at the back of the neck, the cheeks grow ruby-red.

Even Fallon got to like Krystle – perhaps not exactly *love* her step-mother the way the blonde Mrs Carrington might have liked – and Blake whom we were told could be extremely nasty (didn't he have his chauffeur beaten up at one stage?) always seemed so pleasant and urbane.

The writers thought they had an answer to that – they got billionaire Carrington on a murder charge. But that didn't really work. How could it? Only the dumbest of viewers could imagine that he wasn't going to get off the charge. After all, would a series aimed at showing that middle-aged was beautiful allow its leading man to languish in a cell on death row and eventually take that long, slow walk to the Chair? Only if they were planning to electrocute the show at the same time.

No, putting Blake on trial for shooting his son's male lover meant he was plainly heading for an acquittal. That wasn't enough to keep the ratings high.

So that was why the writers decided to bring in another woman – a step that quite clearly wasn't aimed at giving Linda a great deal of pleasure. And indeed it did not. When she heard about it, Miss Evans was furious.

The news was about as bad as it could be for her.

The woman, the writers decided should come into *Dynasty*, was going to be a resurrected first Mrs Carrington, one who, while not trying to claim her ex-husband, was going to make her successor feel very uncomfortable. She would make it clear that Krystle was a usurper in her bed, and one who wasn't exactly perfect in her role as lady of the Denver manor. In short, there was going to be all the bitchiness they thought the viewers could take. And that was generally reckoned to be a very great deal.

Without knowing who this adversary would be, Linda was appalled.

There was no doubt that the woman they were planning to bring in would be a rival for her stardom as well as for the husband in the script. The usurper, after all, would have to be of equal status to have any effect.

After all those years she had spent searching for the part that would make her a big star, a real leading lady, Linda Evans now risked seeing it all snatched away.

Spelling, the executives and the Shapiros now took time off to reassure her. Linda would remain the star. The billing would show that. Whoever it was who was going to play Madeline would be billed as a guest artist.

Linda felt unhappy, as well she might. But no one had given her authority to decide who else would be in *Dynasty*. Until that moment, she wouldn't have considered wanting it. Now, though, it was different and there wasn't a thing she could do about it.

It was a situation to which she would have to become used. Before long, Madeline would become Alexis, a name that was considered to be somewhat more sinister. So, it would soon appear, was the presence of the woman who would play her.

To give her credit, Linda made no further moves against the decision and went around saying how close she and her rival were in real life. But were they? The 'other woman' was Joan Collins.

Not that everyone at first knew that it *was* Joan Collins. Not even Joan Collins herself.

All the public saw was a veiled woman wearing a white suit in the final episode of the first series. The woman was an extra. Who would get the part to fill that suit and hide behind the veil? It had not yet been decided.

When Joan was selected and her identity revealed, the spitting started – not just between Alexis and Krystle but between Alexis and her former husband and between Alexis and practically everyone else.

It was an ironical situation and one that must have been increasingly galling for Linda: the more Alexis spat, the higher the ratings went.

And although women continued to make those nice oohing and aahing noises about Linda's necklines and shoulders, what they said about Miss Collins's wardrobe became one of the phenomena of 1980s-style show business.

There was a different outfit for every scene in which Alexis appeared – evening dresses, dresses she wore at the office she ran, (seemingly, with the same devotion and degree of success as Blake Carrington) dresses for breakfast, dresses for bed (and she was seen to go to bed and take men there, too.)

For a time, it seemed there was a risk of her making Krystle totally superfluous to the story; except that Linda did still have her following and *Dynasty* was now a boat riding a crest of a wave – first in the ratings within months. Nobody in his right TV mind was going to rock that vessel now.

Alexis got more and more nasty – while Krystle got more and more angelic, proving to be the loyal wife, the one who was clearing up after the mess left by her predecessor's mischief. Oh, and what mischief! Suggesting that Blake's children – her children, too, if one needed reminding – were not really his at all. Telling Stephen that she was with him while his father was not. Causing Fallon to have her baby prematurely. And all the time, finding ways to make the whiter-than-white Krystle a little less perfect in her husband's eyes. Blake tells his wife he loves her all the more, they kiss, they embrace, he warms her body (considering how much of it she was exposing – and in the Denver climate, too) and the audience lapped it all up.

'I'm Snow White next to Joan,' Linda joked at the time they first eyed each other in front of a camera.

Both women have since gone out of their way to show how fond they are of each other. And, once the *fait accompli* was established, with Linda continuing to get her star billing and Joan her own individual status at the end of the credits, there was no reason to disbelieve either of them.

Joan received a thundering amount of fan mail for the bitchy Alexis, and relished in being a bigger success than ever before. If Jay Bernstein had been invited to do for the fifty-year-olds what he had done for the forties and the thirties, he would have had no finer product to offer.

As Joan Collins looked beautiful and snarled, men and women everywhere started penning her notes of everlasting devotion.

Linda Evans looked beautiful and whole spoonfuls of butter would have failed to melt in her luscious mouth. But was she holding her own to Miss Collins? Probably not. But that didn't mean that her star was waning. It was a different kind of star and it seemed to be glowing in her own sky - as countless magazine covers were now making very clear. As *Dynasty* got bigger, so did Linda's own drawing power.

She and Joan had been friends for the past five or six years, in the way people on the fringes of the centre of show business inevitably became. Joan had been to the parties Linda and Stan had given. They were in the same group and the same group were constantly meeting, chewing the well-prepared Hollywood fat.

In her best-selling autobiography, *Past Imperfect*, Joan Collins recalls the encouragement that Linda gave her when her stomach was twisted in a series of knots. She said that Linda told her: 'You'll be great. I'm so happy you're doing this part. We all are. Just remember, we were all in the same place and we are all rooting for you.'

Considering that the threat Joan Collins was offering the career of Linda Evans was just as potent as the one that Alexis was making to Krystle, those are generous words indeed.

And Linda seems to confirm it at every available opportunity. 'We're supposed to hate each other,' she told the *Los Angeles Times*, and we have a lot of fun pretending.'

As she illustrated, they played their roles off the set and appeared to enjoy it.

Joan would say: 'What nasty thing am I going to do to you today?' To which Linda would rejoin: 'I don't know. But I'll be ready for you.'

Not particularly witty – the Shapiros hadn't written those lines for them – but the harmless repartee gives something of their true feelings for each other. The fury of a scorned woman for her successor was apparently not allowed to encroach on personal relationships.

It wouldn't be long before both women were slogging it out in a swimming pool, quite the most enjoyable fight since Shirley MacLaine and Anne Bancroft went for each other with handbags flying in *A Turning Point*. It was something of a turning point for Linda. She was shown not to be quite so very, very sweet as people had been afraid she was. When she got out of the pool and straightened out her soaking body, both men and women all over the world cheered. It doubtless had something to do with the Emmy nomination – alas not the award itself – which Linda collected for *Dynasty*.

Miss Evans has said that she is sorry for Miss Collins – a great deal more sorry than Joan undoubtedly is for herself. About Joan, Linda said: 'She does such a good job of acting that, unfortunately, when she goes out in public people are angry with her and they really let her have it verbally.'

As for Linda herself, she was adapting her new life style to the things she had been saying for many years.

There were those who saw Linda as representing the same kind of perfection that Krystle now stood for.

When a huge march was organised on behalf of what America got to know as ERA, the Equal Rights Amendment, Linda was there, wearing out her shoe leather with hundreds of others. She wasn't the only *Dynasty* inhabitant on parade. Her screen husband, Blake, was there, too. John Forsythe didn't think he had much to apologise for. Women had been very good to him, he said that day – appearing for once, minus his blue rinse – and if he could help them by campaigning in some way, then it was only right to do so.

Whether the feminists behind the campaign considered either Forsythe or Miss Evans, with those man-catching clothes and make-up, as the kind of ally they were seeking was somehow beside the point.

Meanwhile, Linda was rejoicing in her own success. She hadn't managed more than a nomination for an Emmy, but there were other awards, important ones, and before now she hadn't had the sort of career that guaranteed these. The Foreign Press Association of Hollywood gave her their Golden Globe. In addition, she won the People's Choice Award for Best Actress in a New Dramatic Series.

But awards or no awards, she still said she had other people to look to, those from whom she could take examples.

She admired the actress Polly Burgen very much – 'because she's a woman who helps other women. She's also operated very successfully in a man's world and yet has stayed very feminine, so she's inspired me to grow in a lot of ways.'

Growing in a lot of ways had long been a Linda Evans desire. She certainly was now doing that, and not just in the breadth of her shoulders.

Most of all, she was becoming more important in the public eye – Miss Collins and Alexis notwithstanding.

In one of the *Love Boat* shows, Linda really had only a guest appearance, but for the first time in her life she was being regarded as close to a superstar as had ever been her lot. The episode was being shot in Turkey and Greece. So far from home, Linda expected to work only when the cameras turned.

It didn't quite happen like that. She was mobbed – by Greeks and Turks who called out 'Kry-stle', 'Kry-stle' wherever she went, in restaurants, in the streets, in markets, in shops and at the hotels she was to visit.

The episode was being shot immediately after the showing of one of Krystle's most traumatic experiences – she had finally succumbed to Blake's demands and not only agreed to sleep with him but, on his instructions, had taken no precautions. She became pregnant and then lost her baby.

(The fault was, needless to say, Alexis's. She fired a gun in the path of Krystle's horse while she was taking an easy ride and caused the animal to bolt. Joan says in her book that she was disturbed about doing this – she didn't think even Alexis could do such a dastardly thing.)

The Greek and Turkish English speakers mobbed her with solicitous inquiries about her state of health. 'My God,' said one woman, 'I'm so glad to see you up and walking around. I was so concerned after you lost the baby.'

Linda said she regarded the inquiry as 'so dear'.

So was the reaction she got from everyone else in Greece and Turkey. In a jewellery store in Athens, she saw a pair of sapphire and diamond ear-rings which, had Stan been along for the ride, she would have said she 'needed'.

The trouble was she had neither cash nor chequebook with her. 'That's all right,' said the man behind the counter. 'You can send me a cheque when you get home.' The man, a dour-looking Greek who seemed to have the cares of the world around his shoulders, was a devoted *Dynasty* fan. Krystle Carrington, he reasoned, would never welch on a deal like this.

It was the summit of her career and of all her hopes for it.

'To me,' she told show biz writer Roderick Mann, '*Dynasty* has provided everything I ever wanted from my career – the chance to do work I love with people I adore.' The money, as has already been indicated, was pretty good, too – and getting better, with subsidiary rights and offers to couple her name with a hundred and one commercial products.

There were problems about that age business. Should she reveal she was forty? That, Jay Bernstein apart, was the difficulty she had to resolve when the birthday actually came around in 1982.

When she took one of her periodic vacations from the *Dynasty* set during its break that year, the forty factor came into focus for the first time.

In a two-part TV mini-series called *Bare Essence*, a story of the perfume business, she was said to have a daughter of twenty. Now that was really laying it on the line. She had to be at least forty to have a child of that age – didn't she? Yes, she admitted, she did.

What she liked most about *Bare Essence* – aside from the fact that she was called Lady Bobbi Rowan – was that she was able to keep her entire wardrobe from the series, just the kind of dresses she loved wearing. They would have fitted into *Dynasty*, too, but those remained the property of Metromedia and ABC.

The part, in an otherwise pretty indifferent mini-series, fitted Linda quite as well as her clothes.

As *Variety* noted: 'Characters, all wrapped in satin and tweeds and furs and pearls, have the depth of those peopling 1930s women's magazine stories without their modesty.... Best thing to be said about the extended telefilm is that it serves as a frame for Linda Evans, who's striking enough to make her role sound intelligent and persuasive – it's not easy. An asset the vidpic badly needs, Evans dominates the proceedings.'

She hadn't had many reviews like that before, but now that previously unknown asset of Miss Evans, her acting ability, was registering.

Linda was confident enough to be independent. Less than two years after the start of *Dynasty*, she fired the man who must be given full credit for his role in establishing the Linda Evans the world believed it knew.

Jay Bernstein was told his services were no longer wanted. He now says he has no bitterness for her. 'She's a nice lady,' he told me. 'I was happy I was able to fulfill her goal.' Which is precisely what he did.

But why the break? 'She seems to be very susceptible to the advice of others – in this case the people looking after her business affairs. They figured they had found a way to save 15 per cent.

'I had counted on her making it big,' he recalled. 'What I didn't count on was that the men who controlled her would encourage her to do it without Jay Bernstein. I have a saying when I begin to feel bitter about events like this – "Once I get a star up to where the air is rarified, they become deified and I become nullified".'

Those who know Linda Evans think that her behaviour towards Jay Bernstein was totally out of character. So his own assessment that she was acting on the advice of advisers must be taken on its face value.

As Bernstein told me: 'Some people have said that without me she wouldn't have got any further than say Linda Gray in *Dallas*. Now everyone is perfect at forty – and we started it. Perhaps they are truthful. I just think that we speeded it up.'

8

Success was really hers. In 1984, Linda was in Rome and was received by the Pope.

Could any achievement be greater than to be recognised by Pope John Paul II? No, it couldn't – except that even Linda confessed the Pope didn't have a clue who she was.

With the little dampener of His Holiness not being a *Dynasty* fan – after all, dynasties don't fit in to the papal way of things – Linda decided not to emulate the pontiff and neglected to kiss the Vatican ground.

It was a strange time for her. The script for *Dynasty* ruled that once again the fictional Krystle was to become pregnant – a state of affairs the real Linda now longed for more than ever. It wasn't likely to happen to her just yet. 'I need to find a man first, don't I?' she laughed.

There were any number on the horizon who might have done her the service, but she didn't think any of them were suitable candidates for a third stab at matrimony. Neither was she in the mood for copying all those other stars who had had children out of what used to be called wedlock.

These days she was living with a society restaurateur named George Santo Pietro, a handsome Latin-looking man just a little younger than she, whose establishments provided pizzas for the wealthy citizens of Beverly Hills.

She had first met him when he drove past her Mercedes car, signalling madly that it was making too much exhaust. He was in a white Jeep.

'He didn't flirt or say anything other than what would be helpful about the car,' she was to recall. (Numerous dealers were suggesting that the most helpful thing to do about her 1971 car was to trade it in, but she said she wouldn't swap it for two Rolls-Royces.)

When they met again, it was two years later and a friend took her to Santo Pietro's restaurant.

They stared at each other. The restaurateur didn't mention *Dynasty*, which is a difficult thing not to do; it is the obvious ice-breaker. He simply looked at her and said, 'Beige Mercedes' and she replied 'White Jeep'.

She was clearly smitten with him and he with her. And he seemed to get on with her new concept of herself. 'He likes an independent woman,' she said. 'I think by nature, I'm happier as a partner. I enjoy being with somebody and sharing my life. But I don't *have* to any more, I *want* to.'

The affair with the restaurateur was to last for the best part of three years and even months after it was all over, they were still seen in each other's company having quiet dinners together. The rumours not only of reconciliation but of marriage were as rife as ever. She denied it. They were ... well ... just good friends.

She was also frequently in the company of make-up artist Lon Bentley, but again there was no talk of marriage: 'I feel I can't go through it again,' she said in May 1985. 'My first two marriages left such deep emotional scars.'

Had she become pregnant with Pietro, it might have compromised her position in *Dynasty* – unless she could guarantee the perfect synchronisation of the biological process with the writing of the script.

Aaron Spelling was now allowing her to take her *Dynasty* clothes home with her, a perk even a woman earning $20,000 a week would appreciate. But she wouldn't want those being made for the pregnant Krystle.

Nolan Miller, the programme's chief wardrobe designer, prepared a whole series of maternity outfits in white linen – draped over the cushions and other padding made for her.

She never spoke about her reservations or frustrated maternal feelings while filming these episodes, but the wistful look in her eyes was noticed by several of her fellow *Dynasty* performers.

She asked Miller how the clothes could be cleaned after an episode when, almost inevitably, they got smeared with make-up.

'Who cares?' he asked – which explained why the budget for *Dynasty* was as high as it was.

The woman who had felt she was doing a service for forty-year-olds now was preparing to do the same for the pregnant. It had been a long time, she said, since pregnant women looked good on the movies or television and she was going to do her best to change that situation.

Eventually, Krystle was delivered of a bouncing baby girl, called – naturally enough – Krystina.

There were constant rumours about the men in her life. The one that she and Richard Chamberlain were in the midst of a steamy affair resurfaced on average once every other month. Linda said she saw the funny side of that, particularly when it was said that the two of them were on honeymoon together. So they used to go to the supermarkets to read the newspaper headlines keeping them informed on how far their romance had gone.

'Richard told me that while I was in Europe on vacation, I broke his heart,' she joked.

She was having just that effect on certain movie producers. In the spring of 1984, they submitted twenty-seven scripts for her approval. She turned them all down. She enjoyed that – and being able to 'just hang out, go to movies, walk on the beach. Rest is a very valuable commodity.'

So was security. Although, she maintained: 'Security is within yourself. To me, there is no outside security. I know that, if the money went tomorrow, I'd still be fine. That's the wonderful gift you give yourself when you go through things in life that seem impossible or painful. You not only come out all right – you can come out better. Now, if something absolutely dreadful happens to me, I say, "What is the lesson in this?" And even in the midst of its being absolutely dreadful, I have faith that the outcome, whatever it is, will one day be positive.'

She certainly had enough positive things happening to her.

The other work that she was accepting was turning very much in her favour. None of it may have been Shakespeare or the kind of play put on at New York's Lincoln Center, but it was the work Linda wanted to do, the kind that paid a fortune and because of *Dynasty*, was sold all over the world.

She made *The Gambler* in 1984, in which she played a Western saloon singer. Her dresses were the kind everyone expected a saloon singer to wear with lots of black lace over her shoulders. They were the finest the wardrobe department could turn out. The jewels around her neck, big rubies and diamonds, may have had to be paste, but they were the best paste ever made. She wore black stockings that were guaranteed to get the patrons whistling louder than they ever did when ordering another shot of whisky.

Dynasty, as more than one writer at the time noted, was never like this. Her soap opera producers would not have allowed her to climb a mountain in a 118 degree heat, the sweat pouring down that usually oh-so-cool complexion. But, like an heiress riding a bus for the first time in her life, that was precisely what she wanted to happen.

'I've been sweet-smiling Krystle Carrington for so long that I couldn't resist playing a tough lady for once,' she explained. 'I've got a lot to thank (Krystle) for. It just helps my sanity to get away from her for a couple of months.'

You could easily believe her. Her hairdresser, who pushed her hair up with a black ribbon on the crown, had a great deal to do with the completely satisfying picture she conveyed.

She also used a gun – as good as any girl in the wild west since the days of Calamity Jane or at least since Betty Hutton starred in *Annie Get Your Gun*.

Even so, she had certain reservations. 'I loved almost every moment of making that film.' *Almost?* Well, even for her, the heat did get a bit, shall we say, hot.

Although Rock Hudson was seriously ill with AIDS, in 1984 he joined the cast of *Dynasty*, to fall in love with Krystle, much to Blake's disgust.

Although Linda now has everything that money can buy, she still hopes and prays that one day she will have a baby of her own.

All the cast in *Dynasty* enjoy borrowing the clothes designed by Calvin Klein and other top New York couturiers. (*Below*) Linda plays her double, Rita, with Heather Locklear as Sammy-Jo in the background.

With Hollywood friends (*abov*
Jack Lemmon and Jane Fond
and (*left*) with boyfriend
Richard Cohen (1985).

Thousands of women in their forties see Linda as their ideal model.

Linda and Lesley-Ann Down rehearse for *North and South*, ABC-TV's new series of the American Civil War (1985).

She was even seen to sing in the film. She wasn't *heard* to sing, however. Her voice was dubbed. 'I'm just not good enough,' she confessed. But she belted out the number as though there was a microphone trained on her and another girl's voice was added afterwards. It was the only way, she said, of sounding convincing – it had been a maxim of the trade ever since Larry Parks mimed for Al Jolson in *The Jolson Story*. He did it so well, that you could see his adam's apple move, the fur on his tongue. There was no fur on Linda Evans's tongue and no adam's apple was in evidence, but she looked as if she were singing, sure enough.

'I managed to do it in front of one hundred cast and crew without once breaking down in tears.' If that could happen, then she felt she had come a long way. But she admitted she owed it all to that very different woman she played in *Dynasty*.

Not, necessarily, that that was the way the gossips felt about her. To the popular magazines in America and most of the other countries where *Dynasty* played, she and Krystle were one and the same person.

She was the first to admit this.

'There was a time when I actually felt guilty that I didn't live up to the stories the gossip magazines wrote about me,' she said. 'The truth is that I am going out with men who are nobody's business but mine. I am not pregnant, and I'm not broody, either. The way I look at it, I'm three different women. Krystle Carrington when I'm working and Linda Evans when I'm not, and then there's another woman who looks like I do and has the same name, but has nothing whatever to do with the real me. If the public wants to believe everything it reads about her, that's fine but I think the public are a lot smarter than they are given credit for.'

Even though she thought it was 'dear' of those people to worry about her state of health when she 'lost' the baby? Perhaps three years into *Dynasty* had made all the difference to her, too.

And it was continually happening. During the early fights between Krystle and Fallon, there were a score of letters a week from people who couldn't understand how she could allow her step-daughter to talk back to her.

'The hardest part is not smiling and enjoying her as I would like to do because it's so much fun to watch Pamela Sue Martin doing her stuff.'

Soon the problem would be removed. Pamela Sue Martin would leave the series and her character killed in a plane crash – a situation that would mysteriously resolve itself in time for the 1986 series. But for the moment, when people talked of step-daughters, it was Pamela Sue they meant. Meanwhile, the real Linda still had a relationship with her own step-daughter Sean.

.Sean has said: 'When you needed Linda, no matter what the crisis or how unpleasant it was, she was there.'

It was a kind of feeling which surprised most of the people who came into contact with them. Contrary to fiction and legend, there are a great number of step-daughters who get on well with their step-mothers. But they are mostly in the confines of a stabilised family. Here, though, were step-mother and step-daughter still staying very close long after a second marriage break-up.

What was more, Sean's mother was still living and she had her brother Russ – for whom, though Sean has said he also enjoyed Linda's kindness, the bond was not nearly as strong.

'Sean,' noted Linda, 'couldn't have been more of a child to me than my own.'

Linda and Sean were so close, it mystified most of the people who came into contact with them. Together, they worked on two books, one a volume in which Sean told her story and spoke about her relationship with her father.

John Derek was as amazed by the relationship as anyone else. While still maintaining that, as Linda herself had said so many times, he and his ex-wife were still the best of close friends, he himself told me: 'My daughter lives in the shadow of Linda and Linda has taken Sean under her wing as though she had given birth to her herself.'

But the book itself – called *Cast of Characters* – pleased Derek much less – since the only person who came out of it with integrity and attractiveness intact was Linda.

As he told me: 'It is the most filthy bit of shit about me. I just can't understand it.'

Linda was more reassuring. As John Derek added: 'Linda says that if I read between the lines, I could see that Sean has shown she really loves me.' Well, Derek was doing just that and not finding any love either above or below the lines.

The second book was a lot less controversial. *The Linda Evans Beauty and Exercise Book* was a best seller wherever it appeared and was serialised throughout the world. In this, she showed how she exercised to keep the various parts of her body trim – including sections which appeared in *Sunday* magazine in Britain on 'Bigger and Better Boobs' – 'Lie on a bench with a weight in each hand' – 'Roll Away That Stubborn Fat' and one simply headed 'Change Your Life'.

The book was intended to show how women could avoid the G-Force – gravity which brought down women's chins, their bottoms, and their busts.

She wrote it because, 'so many women have said to me, "How are you so peaceful inside, how do you manage to look so good?"' She was too shy to describe her feelings to strangers in conversation; she couldn't do it on a TV chat show. But she felt she could do it in a book – even one which didn't make the sort of money she was used to getting. In fact, practically every single author in the world would like to make the money she made from the *Beauty and Exercise Book.*

It really did put on to paper what she believed and did in practice. She added a small gym to her Beverly Hills house, complete with stationary bicycle – it was, she claimed proudly, 'computerised', although what exactly the computer did nobody could really be sure. She rode it for about an hour each morning and used a real bicycle and even jogged whenever she possibly could.

Her favourite hobby remained the one that required a degree less exercise – working in the kitchen.

She said that she liked to cook 'anything that someone

enjoys eating'. Actually, she could be more precise. What she really enjoyed cooking most included crab enchilados, Chinese fried rice, shrimp and chicken in a garlic butter and mushroom sauce. (Her gym was to undo some of the effects of sampling those dishes herself.)

Linda was planning to write a cookery book – actually her second; the first was given to friends as a gift, now she was being commissioned by a publisher to write another.

When she did get round to having it published it would join the two thousand others she owned. 'I buy two or three a month and read them for fun,' she explained.

There was no mention of dieting in the book. 'We have 40,000 or so diets to choose from already,' Linda explained. 'I'm not interested in adding another. And a diet that works for my metabolism may not work for someone else. My general diet technique is to follow a low-carbohydrate plan.'

Her beauty book laid particular emphasis on what it called 'Inner Beauty', which she told the Fashion '83 section of the *Los Angeles Times*, was a 'process of finding yourself, then loving yourself and being at peace with yourself.' Even unattractive women looked beautiful because they had something in the eyes.

Outer beauty, she admitted, was easier to obtain than the inner kind – thanks to plastic surgery, among other things. 'But it doesn't bring happiness. Knowing yourself, loving yourself, looking for the joy in every day does bring happiness.'

There was certainly plenty of joy *every* day for Linda, if you took notice of the pictures appearing with ever greater frequency in the newspapers and magazines and tried – just tried – to contemplate an income received from a top TV series being shown in practically every country in the world. (Just about the only Western nation that did not show all the series was Israel. The TV network there decided that shows like *Dynasty* and *Dallas* were unsettling to a nation that was being told to collectively put its financial house in order.)

But there was no doubt that Linda looked lovely and women

were continually trying to emulate her in whatever way they could.

As she told *Harper's Bazaar* magazine (under a picture of an enticing-looking Linda wearing pin-stripe trousers and a cream wool sweater with a deep 'V' outlined in black under her leather and sheepskin coat): 'Forty Is Fabulous'.

Certainly, it did seem that way to her. What she didn't like, she told the magazine, was to be considered intimidating to other women. 'I have no interest in threatening other women,' she maintained. 'I like them. I grew up with two sisters – we're still very close – and I'm not very competitive in anything.'

But then few women could really afford to be competitive with her. There weren't many, for instance, who could afford to wear the cashmere pull-on trousers that retailed for about $268, or her fur sweater – a sweater that was a real snip at $3,400.

What was she looking for in a man – even a younger man? She was being entirely consistent, remembering what had attracted her to John Derek. 'If his eyes are right – they're the expression of the soul, you know - I don't care what's around them.'

Yes, she was convinced she would marry again. But she wasn't going to try to look younger to attract one. 'I don't want a man whose idea of life is an eighteen-year-old girl. I have confidence in life and believe that there's a marvellous man out there who wants something like me.... I'm not interested in trying to look twenty when I reach fifty. Change is part of the ageing process. Wrinkles *are* going to come. There's no sense in fighting it.'

For that reason, she liked the lines around her eyes. They showed how much she had laughed.

But there was still that nagging bit about not having had children. 'I hope and pray to have one, though I think it's unrealistic to expect that I'd have the patience for a large family at this point.'

In another interview, she said perhaps more intuitively: 'I have what most of the world think they want. But most of the world has everything that *I* really want. The family unit has been a dream in my heart all my life. I've thought, "Okay, here you are. You've got so-called everything. But I haven't got anything.... Is fame and fortune going to keep me company when I'm older? Can you talk with fame and fortune at night when you come home from work? Can you do that when you're lonely and you desperately need to talk to somebody or you want to share something good with somebody?" '

It was a theme to which she was constantly returning. Another time she said: 'It's a tremendous gift. I certainly know I have everything most grown women would die for. Yet I go home at night and sometimes I'm very sad and lonely and I think what do I really have if I don't have someone to share it with?'

She still talked of her ambition to be a housewife.

The mind boggled. Linda Evans in a little apron, scrubbing floors, dusting furniture?

But not having a baby in his or her own room was becoming more and more a void in her life of which she was aware.

It may have been her real self talking, or, on the other hand, she may have just been caught in a reflective, sadder mood. It did sound somewhat more realistic, however, than some of the other off-pat comments about the wonderful life that held no regrets for her. Even super-stars had regrets and unhappy moods.

She was beginning to get round to considering adopting a child – if only to stop the constant battering she was getting from well-meaning friends with statements like: 'Quick, quick, quick. Father Time is going to get you.... You're not getting any younger and there are a lot of younger girls out there after all the guys – *you* should know that.'

Her home, however, would really have seemed to represent most people's ideas of a woman's paradise – all fifteen rooms of it.

The brick and wood house was 'perfect' because it was only twenty-five minutes from the *Dynasty* studios, but as far as she was concerned a spacecraft's distance from the life of a big TV star. The house was practically in the heart of the country, with an entryway containing lots of old-looking pieces of wooden furniture, a grandfather clock, a wooden bench and wood sculpture. She brought in decorator Barbara Wisdom to formulate the exact look she wanted for what she would consider perhaps the most important part of the house, its shop window.

Linda was a collector of oriental porcelain, which she began assembling during a trip to Japan. It was all on view, piece after valuable piece, in her pastel-painted living room with highly polished floors.

The house was thirty years old but the impression it gave was of something somewhat older.

It was, she said, her first real home, and was decorated with the things *she* liked, not those that pleased other people.

Security decreed that she had to have electric gates.

The blue kitchen with its corner dining table, its stove – like a range from the turn of the century – the assemblage of rough-looking wood, gave an 'olde-world' touch to it all. It was just the atmosphere in which she herself liked preparing for her dinner parties. Up to thirty people could be seated at affairs, in a series of small tables in a room off the main dining room.

She only had one live-in maid. Linda wasn't going to repeat the farce she had experienced with servants during the time she was Mrs Stan Herman.

The dining room itself had a mixture of antique English and French furniture.

Her bedroom was the epitome of femininity one might have expected – floral bedspread with a matching chair and stool and close to the bed, a gilt statue of a Buddhist monk in prayer. Above the fireplace in the room – which was rarely, if ever, used, considering the weather in Beverly Hills – hung a portrait of the young Linda, a gift from Barbara Stanwyck.

Linda would say that her favourite place in the house was the den, with its bright loose-covered couch and cushions around the fireplace. She was helped by the top people's designer Mary Ann in selecting the furnishings and pictures in the room.

She also had a billiard room – which was there mainly for the amusement of dinner guests. Even if she were a billiards fanatic – which she wasn't – she wouldn't have had time to use it. In fact, she didn't have time for much, apart from her tennis and her cycling.

'My friends think I have gone off to another planet. I have had to give up a lot, but you can't just spend the rest of life playing.'

Anything missing? No, of course not – and naturally there was that principal requirement of Hollywood-style living – a swimming pool close to the living room and in a corner of the acre of ground on which the house stood. The pool didn't particularly impress her. 'Out here, it's like saying you have a bathroom,' she joked.

Again, one was tempted to think that that was just another symptom of being super-rich. Compared to the Carringtons – and even Linda herself was tempted to make just those comparisons – she wasn't that at all. 'I'm very happy without having so much. With money, there seems to be a burden; the more you have, the more you need. Everyone's trying to get a little more or beat his record or top someone else. There just doesn't seem to be a peaceful place – and me, I like my life peaceful.'

To be fair, that was how she was spending it and there didn't appear to be many people who were stopping her – Joan Collins apart. What seemed to upset Linda most about her relationship with Alexis on screen was the way they had their televised upsets.

La Collins 'adores the verbal confrontations,' she told *Us* magazine. 'But it makes me sick everytime I have to yell at her. I'd rather fight it out. When it came time to do our real fight scene, Joan got sick. And I teased her. "You can't get out of this because I'm going to get you".' And she did. Before the referee could call 'Out', viewers were certain Krystle was the winner.

She seemed to be the winner in so many fields too, outside the series.

Of course, there was a lot of interest in what she was saying. Wasn't she, after all, a symbol? In a way she was protesting that she couldn't understand what all the fuss had been about.

'Men are always accepted as in their prime in their forties and fifties and I don't know why women aren't allowed to be. There are a lot of terrific ladies who are in that age bracket. If women who are my age are able to understand they don't have to give up, that they can have hope and they can work on themselves, it is terrific. If women don't mentally give in and they do something to take care of themselves – go to the gym and work out, take care of their skin, and have the right frame of mind, they'll look great.'

Providing, that is, men didn't always look at a woman's feet. Linda was indeed fortunate she wasn't born in China, where a woman's feet are still considered her finest features. Linda has bunions – and agrees she looks terrible in sandals. And if she wore them, they would be size eight and a half.

All the time, though, writers were concentrating on her beauty and her age. What about her acting? On the whole, comparatively little was being said about that. And that was why the Golden Globe she had been awarded for *Dynasty* had been so important. Even she, too, doubted her acting ability. 'I always thought I was getting away with something,' she conceded.

She also gave a lot of credit for what she was doing in the series to the writers, particularly to Richard Shapiro – his wife Esther worked on ideas with him; Richard did most of the actual writing. 'When I talk to Richard Shapiro after I read the scripts, I'm amazed by how this quiet, shy man writes the most sinfully, wonderfully outrageous dialogue,' she joked.

What seemed particularly agreeable to the girl born Linda Evanstad in middle America was the way watching the series seemed to transcend class barriers. Everyone was tuning in to *Dynasty*.

There was, for instance, the time she agreed to meet writer Phyllis Battelle of *Ladies Home Journal* at the plush Beverly Wilshire Hotel in Beverly Hills. She was doing the Linda Evans best at being incognito – according to Miss Battelle, 'with her face in shadows and her grey-blonde hair tucked under a wide-brimmed hat.'

A man at a nearby table managed to break through the disguise. 'Do forgive me, Miss Evans,' said the stranger, 'my name is Elliott Roosevelt and my wife and I just wanted to say how much we admire you.'

That from the son of the World War Two President made Linda realise just how much of a public figure she had become. 'Goodness sakes,' said Linda. Goodness sakes indeed. When she was a tiny baby in Hollywood, Elliott Roosevelt was a member of America's 'Royal Family', in the papers almost daily, and now he was paying her court. Goodness sakes!

It wasn't just distinguished strangers who made her a Top Person. *Us* magazine named her its favourite sex symbol.

'It seemed so funny to me,' she commented. 'I have these broad shoulders and was always such a skinny person.'

Everyone noted Linda's reluctance to accept that she looked rather special and failed to understand it. Her hairdresser Cherie described her as 'the most secure, most confident woman I have ever worked for' – and could speak with the experience of one who had attended to the coiffures of Doris Day and Lana Turner among a host of other top stars.

Everywhere she went, people didn't just go up to her, like Mr Roosevelt, and say how much they admired her, women would approach her furtively – just to try to squeeze her hand, or perhaps to take a close glimpse at her complexion or have a whiff of whatever perfume she was wearing at the time.

The way Linda responded to those approaches said a lot about her attitude to life and her place in it. As Cherie also noted: 'She sees good in everybody. She never felt better than anyone else. That's why she treats her fans so well. Sometimes, I have to tell her, "Linda, you're the star" because otherwise she ends up carrying my make-up kits.'

There were other examples of being sorted out as someone special. Naturally, an ideal choice for TV commercials. In a way, she was back to the beginning of her career. Except that people were making a lot more of what she was doing for *Clairol* shampoos than had ever been made of her *Canada Dry* advertisements. True, Linda was no longer the ideal dancing partner at teenage parties, but there were any number of compensations.

A luxury hotel in Florida – the Bonaventure Inter-continental – had Linda as their front woman, and a very impressive front woman she was! She hosted an international celebrity tennis tournament there – and all those taking part were told that Linda had been selected for the job because she was the perfect demonstration of 'glowing health and beauty'.

When a diet drink called *Crystal Light* was developed, who better for this Crystal than Krystle? But the summit of her commercial career came in time for Christmas 1984 with the release of a new perfume. *Forever Krystle* left no one with any doubt that a woman called Krystle would be using it until her dying day.

It was marketed by the famous Charles of the Ritz company and created *for* her by the man who had devised the *Opium* line for Yves St Laurent. Usually, women who are asked to identify themselves with new perfumes do so only after the fragrance is established; Linda was invited to help select the essences before it was actually developed.

She had always been a perfume type – ever since a boy had given her a bottle of *Joy*, which she then wore until she became established. Then she graduated to *L'Air Du Temps* when she wanted something light or *Calèche*, when she was in a more sophisticated mood. But now, she was saying she would wear *Forever Krystle* – for ever.

Not that people only wanted to enjoy her perfume. She was in great demand on TV chat shows – on practically every kind of show. When, in 1984, veteran comedian George Burns celebrated his 100th birthday on a television spectacular – actually Burns was 12 years premature since he was then a mere 88, but what was the point of waiting? – Linda came along to pay her tribute. She wore a deeply plunging neckline into which George couldn't help peering even if he hadn't wanted to (he gave no impression of not wanting to, in fact both his eyes seemed to be enjoying the experience thoroughly), and told him how much she admired him. Mr Burns, who was in the habit of escorting young girls to Hollywood functions, doubtless told her before they went on that she was a little old for him.

But there *were* more vital things in her life.

She was still seeking the perfect religion. Even meeting the Pope hadn't convinced her that the Catholics had everything. 'I still like to sit in church ... but there are certain things the Church says that I don't agree with – they are man's version of God. So I try to find God in ways that are more comfortable to me – in meditation, in being with people who are laughing or crying. The God in my life is a joyful, loving, peaceful God.'

If one excluded that desire of hers to have a family, one had to conclude that He was also a generous one. Each success in her notably successful life seemed to breed another. *The Gambler* was so successful that it begat *Gambler II*.

The wardrobe again was about the most expensive she had ever had. But she was to say it was also the most clau-strophobic – 'With dozens and dozens of hooks and buttons and tons of petticoats. The shoes were the kind people really used to wear, very heavy and clumsy. It takes you about half an hour to get into the costume and when you do, you want to get out fast. And all the time we were out there the tem-perature was over 120 degrees. I don't even like to think about it.'

She had a touch of sunstroke while making the film and fainted a couple of times, but she seems to have laughed it off and then got on with the work.

The money for *Gambler II* wasn't bad either. She earned half a million dollars for the role (and at the same time signed a new contract with more money, of course, for *Dynasty*. This one was for four, instead of the previous two, years). But *Gambler II* she liked because it was so different from *Dynasty*.

The show worked so well that a third one was on the way.

Ken Kragen, the producer of the piece, was sure that Linda

was perfect casting, as much as anything because she was such a complex person – much more complex than most people gave her credit for being.

'There are a lot of layers to Linda and most people never get past the top one. If she's displeased with something, I'll never hear it from her. Everything will be going along fine and Linda will be cheerful. Minutes later, I'll hear from somebody, "Linda's very unhappy".'

But how long was it all going to last? She pretended it mattered not at all. Well, if that was so, it mattered a great deal to her two sisters.

Kate, formerly Kathy, was the star-struck one. She wouldn't leave a reception to which Linda had taken them to meet all the ABC stars. 'You're so popular now,' Kate told her star sister. 'What if you're not, next year? We won't ever see this again.'

'I never take for granted that I'll stay on top,' she says. 'I don't know what's going to happen, but I do know it's not going to last for ever.'

9

Isn't anything wrong with Linda Evans?

When Mary-Ellen Banasher asked that in *McCalls* magazine in November 1983, it was such a good question that it was almost obvious.

Linda was, as Jay Bernstein had told me, 'a nice lady.' Indeed that seemed to be everybody's view but as *McCalls* noted and Joan Collins herself had asserted, 'the public is more fascinated by wicked women than it is by the girl next door.'

If that was so, why was this magazine, why indeed was a string of magazines, so keen on writing about her? The answer was simple: After all those years, Linda Evans was the 1980s' model of a film star. Not just a television star, not a super star or any of those terms that are thrown up with every edition of a tabloid newspaper, but a film star the way that Loretta Young or Linda Darnell or Grace Kelly had been.

For once here was a star who didn't have to be a great actress, a devourer of men or the centre of a lurid scandal to get people talking about her. That was the way it was in the Hollywood of the big studio days and that was the way it was again. Linda Evans was the body and face which launched one hundred million admirers.

'I do seem to have a lot of devoted fans and that pleases me enormously,' Linda told *McCalls*.

Linda's clothes continued to amaze, which in itself was another definition of stardom. She wore things that didn't automatically strike people as straight out of the *Dynasty* mould.

When she went to meetings – perhaps to discuss a new contract in the winter or early spring – she wore a suit in turquoise suede ('Business-like but not dull and the colour says I know my own mind.')

She was often in a suede mood, which was why she liked honey and peach separates in suede, sometimes topping it all off with a 1930s cowboy hat.

But it was the evening dresses that enchanted people, or rather which she hoped would enchant them – and she wasn't usually wrong. A red chiffon ('the fabric is so filmy and it moves so beautifully') dress made her feel romantic.

And for those dinner parties? Silky pale hostess pyjamas.

Even casual *Dynasty* watchers noted that her dress style was changing on screen. As her character changed and grew stronger so did the clothes. That was when the necklines started to plunge ever deeper. The shoulders – and she really does have strong wide shoulders – became more exaggerated.

Sometimes, the hips were exaggerated, too. Unlike most women – certainly of her age – Linda was continually trying to make her hips seem bigger. 'They're like a boy's,' she would say deprecatingly. There were those who would dispute that.

Clothing her wasn't simple. After all, who could possibly find the perfect creation for someone so fussy, so well known, so much on view as Linda Evans? Even when she wanted new ear-rings, Cartier had to try to create a style for her – and then take it to the house for approval. It wasn't often these days that she could go into a shop and tell someone 'I really *need* these.' The truth was that Linda Evans didn't really need anything – apart from that baby.

The people she admired most weren't all the obvious ones. Audrey Hepburn had always been somewhere high on a pedestal. When they met at a dinner party in Italy, Linda couldn't get over the fact that she was spending the evening in the company of her idol.

What she would say as the 1980s went into their second half was that she was firmly sure of herself: 'I was pretty unconscious most of my life. I had a lot of love in me and I liked people, so I went stumbling around through life not seeing a lot of things. That was fine for one part of me, but I think being involved in life and taking responsibility for yourself is a much more exciting way to live.'

There weren't many people who would disagree with that. If there was one person in this part of the world who seemed to know where she was going, it was Linda Evans – '*Dynasty's* Gorgeous Gold Bricker', as *Los Angeles* magazine put it.

People were always thinking of new ideas for her – like pairing up with the rival Linda from the rival show. Linda Gray from *Dallas* met Linda for a joint cover feature in *Us* magazine. Both arrived at the magazine's studio complete with wardrobes and personal assistants and spent hours in the make-up rooms before actually facing the cameras.

'A close associate advised me not to do this,' Linda Evans admitted. 'I didn't need to share a magazine cover with anyone.'

Linda herself didn't agree. 'Are you kidding?' she rejoined. 'This is a wonderful idea, showing two women in such a friendly way. It's so positive.'

But what about romance – the real kind that got the gossips salivating?

Her restaurateur and her make-up artist were replaced by an actor – the hunky Tom Selleck, star of the *Magnum* TV opus. Would this be a marriage of the Soaps (if one were allowed to stretch a point and call a private-eye series a Soap)? No, it wouldn't. Nor would it be a marriage between Linda and Tom.

There was a lot of talk that Krystle and Blake were going to split up. Who would be her new TV lover? When people spotted her in restaurants with Selleck, it seemed that he might be the answer, but he wasn't. He was, it seemed, yet another of her 'just good friends'. And dear old dependable Blake wasn't going to be dropped – what would happen to the dynasty then? – any more than was Linda herself, to say nothing of Joan Collins.

Sometimes, the enthusiastic speculation reached unacceptable proportions. In London, the *Daily Mirror* had to apologise to a man it claimed was now engaged to Linda. Within days, the *Mirror* was admitting that he had been happily married for the past fifteen years and had two children.

The media were on safer – but still no more correct – ground with Richard Chamberlain. The former *Dr Kildare* star was linked with Linda's name so frequently, he was almost an honorary member of the *Dynasty* staff. Then in April 1984, came the certain announcement that the following Easter Sunday, Linda and Richard would splice the knot. The day came and went and apart from the number of times they were seen walking down the shadier parts of Sunset Boulevard hand in hand, that was the end of the speculation.

'They are made for each other,' said an American psychologist. But that was as far as it went.

Everybody was getting in on the act. John Forsythe was caught in an off-screen moment with an off-the-cuff remark. 'We really do get worried about her,' he said. 'It's a cruel irony that one of the most beautiful and desired women in the world should have no one.'

John and his wife had an almost parental interest in her. They invited her to their home in the evenings – 'to make sure I don't stay alone all the time,' Linda explained. 'They call me up, take me out ... if it wasn't for them I don't know what I'd do.'

That wasn't what she was saying most of the time. On other occasions, she was insisting how much she enjoyed her life style.

She went to China for another *Love Boat* episode accompanied by John Forsythe, Lee Majors, and – proving just how much she did care for her predecessors – Ursula Andress. And people still wondered whether she was going to find a man. Others concentrated on the meeting of the Dynasties – Ming and TV.

That, too, was part of being the kind of star she was. Old show biz traditions were being revived – like the famous one of top vaudeville entertainers like Al Jolson or Sophie Tucker having cornbeef sandwiches named after them in the Broadway delicatessens. With Linda it was a little more sophisticated. Some of the dishes she had created were being offered in the Ryans Place restaurant – all named after her.

More satisfactory, probably, were the times she was invited on to other shows, like *Glitter*, a series that lived up to its name but had practically nothing else to commend it.

One episode had a mystery cover subject. At the beginning of the show, you saw only the legs of the woman. Then the body. At the end, panting viewers were let into the secret. It was Linda Evans. Actually, it wasn't Linda Evans. The legs were those of actress Anna Leigh London. The body was of Quin Kessler. 'Two years ago,' explained Miss Kessler, 'I met Linda and she agreed we looked alike.' Quin was twenty-five.

The foot-and-leg model sounded as though she was about to be served her lunch in a saucer: 'I have tiny legs and feet that don't look anything like Linda's. I have a size four foot. Linda is a beautiful woman but I think her feet are size eight or eight and a half.' Yes, and she also has bunions, but was that any reason to say so? The *Glitter* producers must have been as pleased about that as Linda was herself.

Meanwhile, there were still the demands of the commercial-makers. Previously, she had been getting $750,000 to appear in TV adverts. Now she was putting up her price to a million dollars. And the offers still poured in like an opened bottle of *Canada Dry*.

She was very keen on the right image, not just for herself but also for the show. 'When people think of *Dynasty*,' she told *Time* magazine, 'they think of elegance.'

Twentieth Century-Fox's licensing company decided they could capitalise on that image and launched the *Dynasty* TV Collection, items they thought symbolised the costumes in the series. Not just dresses which Linda had worn, but also bed linen, shoes, and jewellery priced at anything between $500 and $20,000 a throw.

As *Time* noted, 'Nothing sticks to the Carringtons, so why should this stuff?' That, too, was a demonstration of how far the whole crowd had gone. They could indulge in crass commercialisation and still come up smelling like *Forever Krystle*.

In April 1985, Linda was voted America's Most Beautiful Woman – in a poll conducted solely among women.

She was extending her range. In the autumn that year, she had a one-woman show at Carnegie Hall, New York, an auditorium which over the years had witnessed a great many marvellous performances – mostly musical. Linda depended on her physical appearance and a script specially written for her.

She didn't either sing or dance – although that was precisely the way it could be said she reacted to a couple of events that spring and summer.

10

Being Linda Evans was proving as tough as it was exciting. And only because she was who she was.

While she gained from the attention *Dynasty et al* brought her – fabulous wealth, tremendous public adoration – the inability to live a normal private life undoubtedly took its toll, sometimes in ways that the average person would not have conceived possible.

Those electrically-controlled iron gates were not sufficient protection against uninvited guests, for instance. In fact, things got so bad that in March 1985, she gained a court order preventing an unmarried black girl from pestering her. That was unusual, even for a big star.

Few people knew for sure Linda's Beverly Hills address, but Joann Bratcher found out and, as a result, Linda complained she was 'wrecking' her life.

Bratcher appeared one day and wouldn't go away. When she left, it was only the end of the first of her unwelcome visits.

She came dozens of times – and before long was telling Linda's staff that she was her long-lost sister (colour having nothing to do with it.)

The woman got into the house on one occasion, saying she was Linda's 'black angel'.

In a deposition to Santa Monica court, Linda declared: 'One night there was a knock on the door and when I opened it, it was this woman. I demanded that she leave and slammed the door in her face. This woman has been making my life intolerable. I called the police department and had her removed.'

And she went on: 'This woman's constant arrivals at my house, her refusal to leave and her incoherent letters have caused great emotional distress. I am afraid to be alone in my home.'

So afraid, that she demanded her secretary stayed at the house with her at night.

One of the *Dynasty* directors, Curtis Harrington, described how she looked behind her all the time she was working on the set. She is nerve-racked,' he said.

The woman had rung Linda's doorbell in the middle of the night, and spent hours sitting outside the house. The police said there was little they could do, short of getting a court order.

Finally, the court issued a restraining order against Bratcher.

It was, Linda said, 'the most bizarre and frightening experience of my life'.

Not quite. A short-term newcomer to the *Dynasty* set was Rock Hudson, who was for years the epitome of Hollywood beefcake, the man voted by millions of girls as the one they would most like to spend a night with, and so long the partner of Doris Day in all those frothy comedies like *Pillow Talk* and *Lover Come Back*.

Hudson had been seriously ill and looked it. He was practically skeletal and it took some time before he would be recognised – an unfortunate state of affairs for any star – by *Dynasty* viewers. He played one of Krystle's old flames – much to Blake's disgust.

Their relationship was fairly innocent, but they did kiss each other.

Then he had to be written out of the show. He was too ill to carry on. Nobody suspected very much, until it was revealed that Hudson was in hospital in Paris – suffering from AIDS.

Now, there were thousands of people who knew that Rock Hudson was a homosexual, but until this announcement, it never got any public exposure. Suddenly, he was being seen as a standard bearer for fellow 'gays' and when he declared he was suffering from AIDS, the statement was greeted sorrow-fully by practically everyone – and seen as an extraordinarily brave gesture by others (including Elizabeth Taylor) which heightened the tragedy of the newly-discovered syndrome.

His friends were distraught. But nobody was more so than Linda. She *had* kissed him and there were all sorts of stories about the danger of picking up AIDS from the saliva of known victims.

Linda was so disturbed that she talked about it.

When Rock got to hear about her disquiet, he made a public apology to her – in a brief moment of lucidity from what turned out to be his deathbed.

He had, he said, been 'plagued with guilt' ever since he discovered how upset Linda had been. 'If I could, I would crawl on my hands and knees to Linda's side to plead for her understanding and forgiveness,' he went on. 'I am sorry for the hurt and anxiety I brought her. I prayed she would never know what was wrong with me.'

It was the last statement that angered Linda and her advisers most. It gave the impression that he had tried to hide and then get away with an act which he *knew* could have disastrous consequences.

Friends were reported as saying that Linda was 'scared to death', even though she was constantly being reassured that she had little to worry about.

Actually, things were not quite so cut and dried. Doctors debated with each other as to whether kissing could cause the AIDS virus to be passed on. Then there was doubt as to whether Rock did, in fact, make the statement at all. A plea for more to be done for AIDS victims and the announcement he had the disease himself was later said not to have come from Rock at all but from his publicist.

Linda would say that the apology was genuine. Hudson was supposed to have added: 'She had so much obvious respect and affection for me and she wanted so badly for us to be good together in all our scenes, I just kept quiet.'

But he emphasised that he had consulted his doctors before

doing the kissing scene and they had assured him he would be presenting her with no danger.

'I told Linda I was just a little under the weather. She would bring cookies and stuff like that trying to fatten me up.'

She issued a statement wishing Rock and all other AIDS sufferers 'courage and strength'.

Even after Rock Hudson's death in the autumn of 1985, Linda was showing evidence of the strain under which she felt.

There were two ways of looking at what had happened. On the one hand, she was feeling terrible and was having great difficulty in keeping her anxiety to herself. On the other, was it dangerous to her career talking about all this?

She was advised that it was and so came out with a statement which gave the impression that she really wasn't concerned at all.

It convinced few people, especially those who knew her. But now Linda was saying: 'I want to assure my fans that doing the sequence did not in any way endanger my life. I have not been concerned about my health at any point.'

The *Dynasty* producers invited their cast to take blood tests to reassure them. Linda's was clear. She re-emphasised 'Quite simply,' she said, 'people should not be worried about my well being because I am not the slightest bit worried myself. I'm sure you can't catch AIDS through casual contact like kissing.'

But the worry did linger. Just before Christmas 1985, friends were saying that she was showing many signs of her anxiety.

But there were other concerns for her, too – and one of them to do with *Dynasty*, in which it began to appear that Joan Collins was finally getting the upper hand. It was all very well being the goody-goody, but La Collins's outrageous wardrobe and her superb make-up made her the one the viewers were talking about – and slightly fewer viewers at that. *Dynasty* was finally beginning to drop in the ratings.

All this was happening at just the time a sequel was being released, *Dynasty II – The Colbys* (about the family into which Joan Collins was supposed to have married briefly but wealthily at the time of her entry into the series). It starred Charlton

Heston and – here the wheel was spinning again – Barbara Stanwyck.

To give Krystle more bite, it was cleverly – so the writers and producers thought, but it went on for too long and never really convinced anyone – arranged for Linda to play a double role, Krystle and a woman who would take her place. This woman would dress like Krystle, eat like Krystle and make love like Krystle (although she tried to get away from that; adding a sleeping powder to Blake's pre-bedtime brandy every time he appeared to show an interest in treating her as a wife.) It all got far too boring.

And the 'real' Krystle? She was being kidnapped and knocked about by none other than that well known advertisement of American suntan lotions, George Hamilton, who had looked a great deal happier playing Dracula.

If Krystle showed remarkable fortitude on screen, the real-life Linda Evans was a lot less sanguine.

One day she burst into tears on the set. 'Why don't you just kill off Krystle?' she demanded. 'You're killing me.'

Indeed, it almost seemed like that. While the mythical Krystle was in the process of being raped, the real Linda Evans was knocked unconscious on the set. She was supposed to be struggling with Mr Hamilton – and had turned down the offer of a double for the scene. He got rougher – which the script instructed him to do – she banged her head on the ground and was knocked out cold.

Linda was ill at home for a week, suffering from concussion.

But this was as nothing compared to the emotional turmoil of yet another romance. Friends had been talking for months about the possibility of her teaming up with Tina Sinatra's former husband Richard Cohen.

They were seen together at all the best places – that is, the kind of places she had been seen with John Derek, Stan Herman and George Santo Pietro. Only this time, an announcement was actually made – and everything about it seemed official. No date was mentioned, but both parties said they were engaged to each other.

Millionaire Mr Cohen told everyone he was giving her a new $10 million house.

It all made a change from her previous state. Only a few months before, at the 1985 Golden Globe award ceremony, she had appeared on her own. 'Nobody,' she said at the time, 'wants me'.

She was under analysis. Even her therapist was said to have been asked by her to find 'a decent man'. There were still constant offers of marriage – some of them from fairly important, high-powered men in the picture business, none of whom she knew. So the letters were thrown away. When a Los Angeles cab driver got love sick, she called the police and the man was sacked.

He had been given the job of taking Linda to and from the studio in his employers' limousine. Instead of confining himself to talk of the weather or the state of the dollar, he confessed undying love for her. Linda answered by closing the sound-proof glass screen separating the front and back seats. When he began pestering her outside his working hours, the police were brought in.

All this, she thought, would end when she married Cohen. And she couldn't contain her excitement. She declared: 'I have gone from being the loneliest woman in Hollywood to being the happiest. I never thought I would fall in love again. Richard is charming, bright and witty. I'm so glad our friendship has blossomed into romance.'

There did seem a certain consistency in her choice of prospective husbands. Cohen was about the same age as Stan Herman and also Jewish.

And Linda said she was going to quit *Dynasty*. Having a husband and a baby were much more important.

John Forsythe said he was despondent. The show couldn't exist without her. So the matter was forgotten.

Linda contented herself by saying she had never been happier and most of all looked forward to that baby. But it was money that took up most of the attention, it seemed. The lawyers got busy.

Yet before any marriage settlement agreement could be drawn up, the affair was over. Or was it? She and Cohen were occasionally in each other's company, but there was no more talk of a wedding.

David Niven Junior gave them a St Valentine's Day party in February 1986 and said he expected that would be the occasion when the engagement would be formally announced. But it wasn't.

Her greatest problem was trying to separate those two lives of Linda Evans, her own and Krystle's, and keeping up with the requirements of being the show's star.

'I need to be five people to do the things people want me to do. I would be up all night, fixing myself up to look great all day and it's not possible. I finally had to learn to say "No." But it's still not at all easy.'

And she could still be upstaged, as at a televised royal gala before the Queen, Prince Philip and Princess Anne.

The show was in Edinburgh and she and Richard flew into the Scottish capital with Richard's twenty-year-old son, Andrew, in a white private Lear jet (honouring a tradition initiated when Danny Kaye learned to fly one of the planes and subsequently became a vice president of the company). The party were then spirited away to the Caledonian Hotel in a motorcade – a pale blue Rolls-Royce for the people, a Daimler for their luggage. Soon afterwards, she went into her first pub. She wasn't recognised. Was this an omen? She showed no sign of being upset. Besides, there were bigger fish in the Scots sea ...

'To have the Queen in the audience is just wonderful,' said Linda. 'I'm going to be more excited than anyone else in the audience.'

So the show was going to be another meeting of Dynasties, in this case Hollywood's and Windsor's.

If only the Queen was to live up to expectations – or perhaps if only she had lived up to the Queen's.

For this, she had learned an act, and finally agreed to sing and do a dance. The only trouble was that, unexpectedly, she was on screen with the BBC's favourite chat show host Terry Wogan.

She suddenly became tongue-tied, and the couturier dress – which viewers noted gave every impression of fitting so close to her lily-white skin that there was no room for anything underneath - and sparkling diamonds notwithstanding, Mr Wogan took over while she did little more than look embarrassed. That sort of thing didn't happen to Linda Evans very often. In America, it never happened.

Usually, the Queen engages the stars in conversation after a Command Performance, with a big smile every time. She only gave Linda a passing nod. 'Oh, she was cool with her all the time,' said an observer.

Linda felt pretty cool herself. She wasn't allowed to bring Richard to the occasion and he had to content himself with a luxury suite at the Caledonian Hotel.

There was, next day, a garden party at the Edinburgh royal palace, Hollyrood House. Hollyrood, as Linda discovered, wasn't a bit like Hollywood. Again the Queen ignored her, though the Prince and his daughter did make some small chat.

Had Linda done something to offend Her Majesty? No one knew of anything.

It was, though, just a slip on the way. Every path she took in her career seemed to be strewn with roses. The general definitions of a star seemed to be summed up in the personality she offered to her public.

'Fortunately,' she would say, 'I've managed not to get caught up in the Hollywood game. I was never one of the "in" Hollywood people. I'm not that kind of person. I basically have my own friends and my own way of life out of the Hollywood scene. It suits me perfectly.'

In fact, she thought, the only problem with her home was that she wasn't able to spend enough time in it.

That was not to say she was happy or even proud of everything she did. In this she was being very womanly. 'I'm sure I did manipulate to be loved. Sure, we do all sorts of things to be loved, because we're frightened. Now, it's different. I don't *need* a relationship, I *want* a relationship.'

There were those who agreed that a relationship was precisely what she did want.

She said, though, that she was going to stay happy 'because I have finally learned to value myself as a woman.' There were millions of others who seemed to do the same thing – to judge by her fan mail.

'I believe life is a learning experience. We can change our thinking if we can believe and try.'

But she *was* still mystified by all that had gone before. 'I can't believe everything that has happened to me. It's all a miracle.'

So much a miracle that Jay Bernstein told me: 'When I see movies and see people talking about Linda Evans, when I see an ad for the *Los Angeles Times* magazine that has Linda Evans on the cover, I feel rather good.'

She was, in every respect, most people's idea of what Krystle should be, despite the problems that brought. Soon the Perfect Forty-year-old would become the Perfect Forty-Five-Year-Old. But the perfect Woman? Only if she had that baby – and its lack was causing her still the odd moment of unhappiness. If she did have one, there might really be a Linda Evans Dynasty.

Index

ABC, 23, 24, 70–4, 75, 84
Actors Studio, 58
The Adventures of Ozzie and Harriet, 17, 19
L'Air Du Temps, 107
Amsterdam, Morey, 24
Andress, Ursula, 26, 27–9, 30, 42, 44, 46, 51–2, 59, 113
Anne, Princess, 122, 123
Avalanche Express, 51, 61–2
Avalon, Frankie, 24

Bachelor Father, 16–17
Baker, Joy, 47
Balsam, Martin, 46
Banasher, Mary-Ellen, 110
Bare Essential, 91
Battelle, Phyllis, 105–6
The Battle of the Network Stars, 70
Beach Blanket Bingo, 24
Beach Party, 24, 31
Belmondo, Jean-Paul, 27, 28
Bentley, Lon, 94
Berenson, Marisa, 50
Berger, Senta, 22
Bernstein, Jay, 24–5, 26, 68–70, 71, 72, 74, 75, 82, 91, 92, 110, 124
Beta Psi Delta, 10
The Big Valley, 23, 24–5, 26, 30, 33, 38, 65
Bistro, 53
Bonaventure Inter-Continental Hotel, 107

Bratcher, Joann, 116–17
Brennan, Walter, 23
Brotherhood, Ruth, 20
Brothers, Joyce, 68–9
Buchholtz, Horst, 62
Burgen, Polly, 89
Burns, George, 107–8
Burton, Richard, 52
Buttons, 21

Calèche, 107
Campbell Soup, 15–16
Canada Dry, 14–15, 107
Cartier, 111
Cast of Characters, 98
CBS, 79
Chamberlain, Richard, 21, 22, 95, 113
Charles of the Ritz, 107
Charlie's Angels, 73
Cherie, 106
Chilberg, John E., 78
The Circus of the Stars, 82
Clairol, 107
Cohen, Andrew, 122
Cohen, Richard, 120–2
Coldwater Canyon, 65
Collins, Joan, 86–9, 90, 104, 110, 112, 119
Connors, Chuck, 55
Corley, Al, 76
Crystal Light, 107
Cummings, Robert, 24
Curtis, Patrick, 18–20

Daily Mirror, 113
Dallas, 70–1, 75, 79, 80, 100
Dangaard, Colin, 56
Derek, Bo, 37, 41–2, 44, 49, 52, 60, 64
Derek, John, 16, 25, 26–43, 44–8, 49, 51, 52, 57, 59, 60, 75, 98–9
Derek, Russell, 33, 36, 46, 98
Derek, Sean, 27, 30, 32–3, 36, 46, 98–9
Disney, Walt, 23
Dmitri, 51
Dupont, 16
Dynasty, 74, 75–92, 93, 94–5, 96, 97–8, 100, 105, 108, 111, 114, 117–19, 121
Dynasty II—The Colbys, 119–20
Dynasty TV Collection, 114

Edwards-Lowell, 79
Elizabeth II, Queen, 122–3
The Eleventh Hour, 21
Emmy Awards, 89
Equal Rights Amendment (ERA), 89
Evanstad, Alba, 9–10, 12, 13, 18
Evanstad, Carol, 10, 12
Evanstad, Kathy, 10, 12, 109
Evanstad, Mrs, 10, 11–12, 13, 32, 39

Falana, Lola, 52
Fawcett, Farah, 68
Filoli, 78
First Artists, 63
Flair Modelling School, 11
Foreign Press Association, 89
Forever Krystal, 107
Forster, Robert, 55, 58
Forsythe, John, 73, 75, 79, 84, 89, 113, 116, 121
Franciscus, James, 65

The Gambler, 96, 108
Gambler II, 108
Gardner, Arthur, 22
Garner, James, 55
Glitter, 114

The Glory Guys, 22
Gray, Linda, 70, 112

Hagman, Larry, 70
Halliwell, Leslie, 52
Hamilton, Alana, 50
Hamilton, George, 120
Hamlin, Harry, 59
Harrington, Curtis, 117
Hartford, Conn., 9
Harvey, Laurence, 49
Hayley, Jack, 50
Hefner, Hugh, 53
Hepburn, Audrey, 111
Herman, Denise, 61
Herman, Stanley, 48–58, 59–60, 61, 65, 66
Heston, Charlton, 119–20
Hopkins, Bo, 77, 81
Huddleston, David, 52
Hudson, Rock, 117–19
Hunter, 65

Janssen, Dani, 50
Janssen, David, 51, 58
John Paul II, Pope, 93, 108
Joy, 107

Keith, Brian, 23
Kessler, Quin, 114
The Klansman, 52–3
Klein, Anne, 80
Klein, Calvin, 80
Klein, Frances, 51
Kragen, Ken, 108–9

La Scala, 53
Laven, Arnold, 22
Legend At Sundown, 55
Levy, Jules, 22
The Linda Evans Beauty And Exercise Book, 99
Lloyd, Harold, 50
London, Anna Leigh, 114
The Love Boat, 82, 90, 113

McCalls, 110
MacLaine, Shirley, 74

McQueen, Steve, 63–4
Majors, Lee, 113
Malone, Dorothy, 24
Mann, Stan, 91
Mars, 16
Martin, Pamela Sue, 76–7, 79, 98
Marvin, Lee, 52, 62
Mary Ann, 103
MGM, 17, 21
Miles, Vera, 23
Miller, Nolan, 80, 94
Minelli, Liza, 50
Mitchell, 47
Mitchell, Cameron, 52

Nameth, Joe, 62
Niven, David Jr, 122
Northrup, Wayne, 78
Nowhere to Run, 58

Oil, 70–4
Once Before I Die, 27
Once Upon A Time, 41

Paluzzi, Luciana, 52
Parslow, Philip, 79
People's Choice Award, 89
Peppard, George, 73
Peyton Place, 79
Philip, Prince, Duke of Edinburgh, 122, 123
Pietro, George Santo, 93–4
Pips, 53
Playboy, 30, 37, 60
Powers, Stephanie, 10
Price, Vincent, 24
Principal, Victoria, 70
Raffles, Paul, 2, 24
Rains, Claude, 23
Rietty, Robert, 62
Right Bank Upstairs, 53
Robertson, Dale, 77
The Rockford Files, 55
Roosevelt, Elliott, 106
Ryans Place, 114

Sampson, Will, 55
Saxon, John, 46
Schell, Maximillian, 62
Selleck, Tom, 112
Shapiro, Aaron, 84
Shapiro, Esther, 71, 79, 84
Shapiro, Richard, 71, 79, 84, 105
Shaw, Robert, 61
Simpson, O.J., 52
Smith, Cecil, 78
Smith, Mr, 78, 79
Spelling, Aaron, 71–2, 75, 94
Spelling, Candy, 74
Stanwyck, Barbara, 23, 30, 33, 103, 120
Starsberg, Lee, 58
Sun, Patricia, 56
Taylor, Elizabeth, 118
10 (film), 60
Those Calloways, 23
Tom Horn, 62–4, 72
Trader Vic's, 53
Tucker, Sophie, 9
Turner, Lana, 10
Twentieth Century-Fox, 114
Twenty-Twenty, 70
Twilight of Honor, 22

The Untouchables, 17
Us, 106, 112

Volkswagen, 15

Warner Brothers, 62–3
Welch, Raquel, 20
Weld, Tuesday, 10
Wells, Carole, 14
Wildflowers, 38
Winkler, Henry, 82
Wisdom, Barbara, 103
Wogan, Terry, 123
Wynn, Ed, 23

Young, Bunky, 36